# HOUSEPLANT
# BASICS

# HOUSEPLANT
# BASICS

David Squire and
Margaret Crowther

**Sterling Publishing Co., Inc.**
New York

Library of Congress Cataloging-in-Publication Data
Available

10 9 8 7 6 5 4 3 2 1

Published by Sterling Publishing Company, Inc.
387 Park Avenue South, New York, NY 10016
First published in Great Britain by Hamlyn,
a division of Octopus Publishing Group Limited

© 2001 Octopus Publishing Group Limited

Distributed in Canada by Sterling Publishing
c/o Canadian Manda Group, One Atlantic Avenue,
Suite 105, Toronto, Ontario, Canada M6K 3E7

Printed in China
All rights reserved

Sterling ISBN 0-8069-8849-5

# CONTENTS

# INTRODUCTION

A house is not a home without houseplants. Whether the plant is an addition to your home in the form of a pot plant that changes with the seasons or is an old friend in the form of a long-lived plant in a permanent position, it will bring your living space to life.

It may or may not be true that plants respond to being talked to, but they certainly respond to good care. If you are to get the best from your plants, you must be aware of the sort of conditions in which similar plants grow in the wild and try to meet the needs of your plants in terms of compost type, the level of light, the degree of moisture, humidity and temperature in both winter and summer, the amount of fertilizer necessary at different times of year and any other specific requirement they might have. In return, they will reward you with strong growth, a good shape, healthy leaves and beautiful flowers. And whether or not plants respond to people except by flourishing when well cared for, people certainly respond to plants, and feel better for their presence in the home.

Choosing houseplants needs as much care as buying any other item for a home. The plant needs to fit in with its surrounding as well as to create an attractive display in itself. It is essential to buy healthy plants that will last. Buying an inexpensive plant that dies within weeks is a waste of money. Check before buying, and discard plants with roots coming out of drainage holes, those with wilting leaves, any plant with signs of pest and disease and those where the compost and pot are covered with moss or slime. Also avoid plants that are displayed outdoors in hot sunshine or in draughts.

Getting plants home quickly and safely and acclimatizing them to indoor life is also important. Make sure that the garden centre or nursery wraps up the plant to protect it from draughts and to reduce the chance of it being damaged in transit. Do not put a plant in your car boot if the weather is extremely hot or cold: instead, stand it upright in a box inside the car. When you get your plant home, unpack it and stand it in a lightly shaded, draught-free place in gentle warmth for about a week. Water the compost. If a few buds or leaves initially fall off, do not worry unduly because the plant is probably just settling down. During this initial period, check regularly that the plant is not infested with pests and diseases.

*Above*: A conservatory
provides the opportunity to
create an indoor garden of
ferns and greenery.

# 1

# HEALTHY HOUSEPLANTS

Most houseplants are undemanding, producing attractive foliage or flowers for several years if given the basics of water, food and light. Routine care need not take much time, but your plants will repay your attention.

*Left*: A sun room provides both ample space and a range of temperature and light conditions that will allow a variety of plants to grow happily.
*Right:* Pink and red *Kalanchoe blossfeldiana* (flaming Katy) add warmth and colour to a collection of foliage plants, which includes a variegated *Hedera helix* (ivy), *Ficus pumila* (creeping fig) and a young *Ficus benjamina* 'Variegata' (weeping fig).

Providing regular water is, of course, vital. Choose a watering-can with a long spout to make watering easy and buy a mist spray so that you can regularly spray with tepid, lime-free water the many plants that need humidity. Standing plants on clay granules or pebbles in trays or bowls of water is an attractive way in which to provide additional humidity.

Keep plants looking their best by cutting off dead flowers with sharp scissors or secateurs and pinching out growing points to keep them bushy or snip them into shape as necessary. Clean the leaves of foliage plants with a cloth wrung out in tepid water. Watch out for pests and diseases, and treat them promptly (see pages 122–23).

When a houseplant fills its pot with roots it is essential to move it into a larger one. If left where it is, the plant's growth will be stunted and its appearance will deteriorate. Repotting provides the plant with further nutrients

and more space for its roots. It also creates a firmer base for the plant, balancing leaf growth and helping to prevent it falling over. At each repotting, move the plant into a pot that is only slightly larger, especially during its early life. In a pot that is too large, the plant is surrounded by too much compost and its roots can become saturated with water, which eventually causes them to decay and the plant to die. Large plants are generally top-dressed rather than being completely repotted.

The clearest indication that repotting is needed is when the plant's roots are growing out of the pot's base. There are other, less obvious, signs, including a general lack of vigour and deterioration in health, caused by the plant being deprived of nutrients. New leaves are small and old ones become increasingly pale and yellow. Also, pot-bound flowering plants produce fewer flowers. In addition, new leaves will have

pale areas between the veins, and they are also likely to hang limply because they are suffering from a lack of moisture.

A healthy, recently repotted plant soon resumes growth, producing young shoots and fresh, brightly coloured leaves. After repotting, place the plant in light shade until growth restarts. This is indicated by the development of fresh shoots. Until then, keeping the plant out of strong and direct sunlight ensures that the need for water is reduced. Position plants with variegated leaves in good light, so that their colours are enhanced. Strong sunlight, however, should be avoided. Plants with uniform outlines should be rotated about 90 degrees several times a week. If this is not done, leaves turn towards the light. Place the plastic or clay pot in an ornamental outer pot (often called a cache or display pot), selecting a colour that harmonizes with the plant.

# types of houseplant

Houseplants come in all shapes and sizes. They may be slow or fast growing, long or short lived, leafy or flowering. From a designer's point of view they can be roughly divided according to their appearance. There are rosette-forming and bushy plants, from small to large, suitable for table tops and windowsills and for arranging in groups. Plants that climb or trail are candidates for hanging baskets, training on screens and up poles, standing on plinths, shelves and high windowsills, or simply, when young, for training up canes or around hoops as windowsill plants. Finally, there are specimen plants of various kinds, from enormous ferns for containers on stands and high display tables to air-rooting climbers for large mossy poles and weeping figs and other plants with tree-like shapes.

Most houseplants are grown either mainly for their flowers or mainly for their foliage, but within these two groups there is a wealth of choice between: seasonal or almost all-year flowering, perfumed flowers, climbing and trailing plants, plants with bold foliage that reward with a burst of flowers, plants whose leaves are as colourful as flowers, plants for sun rooms and conservatories and plants for cool rooms. Certain plants have special status: palms, ferns and bromeliads, cacti and other succulents all have distinctive features of their own, and then there are plants grown for their colourful berries or fruits, tropical insectivorous plants, and, of course, the wealth of flowering plants grown indoors from bulbs.

Although many plants are widely known by their common names, these can vary from country to country, even from person to person. To be sure that you are identifying a plant correctly it is always safer to use its botanical name. Even botanical names may change from time to time, however, and when this has occurred, both the old and the new names have been included to avoid confusion. This is particularly true of both desert and forest cacti, which have been subject to much reclassification in recent years and some of which may be offered for sale under as many as three specific names.

# positioning & displaying plants

Once you have got your plant home and have acclimatized it to your house, you should place it in its permanent position.

## CHOOSING A ROOM

Sitting rooms, dining rooms and bedrooms are places of peace and tranquillity, and have more constant temperatures and fewer draughts than other parts of the home. In sitting and dining rooms plants can be displayed in floor-standing groups, in troughs or in fireplaces, on windowsills and on tables. Large floor-standing specimens in big pots make superb focal points. Bedrooms are often cooler, and so useful for ferns, azaleas, cyclamen and other plants that need slightly lower temperatures. There are many plants for cooler conditions, from impressive ferns to dainty primroses. Unheated spare bedrooms are often the best place in the house for plants that need a dormant period in winter and for growing plants from seeds and cuttings.

The levels of activity and temperature changes in kitchens make them inhospitable for many plants. It is best to reserve the kitchen for inexpensive plants and plants that will not get in the way: easy-care green plants, perhaps hung on wall brackets, and undemanding flowering plants on windowsills.

Bathrooms are also primarily functional places, even though they can also be havens of privacy and comfort. They are often advocated as ideal areas for growing plants that love humidity, but not all bathrooms are humid all the time and the

*Left*: Ferns love humidity and are often displayed in bathrooms. The unusual *Platycerium bifurcatum* (staghorn fern) has quite striking architectural qualities that make it blend well with plain white bathroom fittings and the old-fashioned water taps.
*Right:* This *Exacum affine* (Arabian violet), a small and lightly perfumed plant, is ideal for a pretty bedroom.

temperature can fluctuate widely. Again, it may be better to choose tolerant plants.

Halls, landings and passages can be draughty or have low light levels, and people passing to and fro may brush past leaves or even knock over plants that are not carefully positioned. If there is space, large specimens can stand in corners, trailing plants can hang in baskets, and foliage plants or pot plants can stand on a hall table to create a welcoming atmosphere.

Many flowering plants are fragrant, including some not generally known for their scent, such as some cyclamen, daffodils and the houseplant primroses. Conversely, some plants known for their scent have unscented forms. It is always best to be guided by one's nose. Heavily scented plants, such as hyacinths, hoyas, jasmine and stephanotis, must be carefully positioned. While most people like a gentle fragrance in a bedroom, others find these strong perfumes overpowering. Equally, strongly scented plants

are not ideal for a small kitchen or dining room, while plants such as *Cestrum nocturnum* (night jessamine) give out more fragrance at night and are perfect for a sitting room. Scented plants placed in the hall perfume the whole house and add an extra welcome.

## DISPLAYING PLANTS

There are numerous ways of displaying plants. The simplest is, of course, to stand a single plant alone in its pot, in a place where it gets the right amount of light – usually on a windowsill. But plants often look better – and grow better – when they are in a group. They can be grouped with their pots on show or arranged with the pots hidden in a container, such as a trough, or they may be planted together in a container to form a sort of indoor garden.

Some plants dictate the way in which they should be displayed. The largest plants need large, floor-standing pots, although they do not necessarily have to be displayed as single

specimens. A group with an architectural plant such as a palm as its main element, grading down through large and medium-sized foliage plants and ferns and softened with trailing ivy, can be a stunning feature in a room with high ceilings, plain-painted walls and simple furniture. This sort of arrangement can be enhanced by a large mirror, which will show the entire arrangement from all sides, or by careful spotlighting to create highlights and shadows.

Climbers and trailers must be allowed the space to grow, and a hanging basket or a plant stand is perfect for trailers. Small climbers can be grown up canes or around hoops, and vigorous climbers can be trained over wires or trellis to form room dividers, to obscure an ugly view or to adorn a conservatory wall.

.Moisture-loving, draught-fearing plants can be planted together in a glass terrarium, bottle garden or Wardian case to make a beautiful and interesting centrepiece.

# containers & composts

Most plants are sold in plastic pots and in compost that contains sufficient nutrients to sustain them for several months. However, plastic pots are not especially attractive, and you will either wish to disguise them by placing them inside a more decorative cache pot or by repotting them into something more decorative. You will also, if your plant is to last for more than the first year, have to consider repotting it into fresh compost.

## CONTAINERS
The sizes of pots, measured across their tops, range from 3.5cm (1¼in) to 38cm (15in) wide. For most houseplants, four sizes are sufficient: 6cm (2½in), 8cm (3in), 13cm (5in) and 18cm (7in), although large, floor-standing

plants may need a 25cm (10in) pot. There are complementary saucers available in which pots can be stood.

Clay pots are traditional containers for plants. They create a firm base and harmonize with most leaves and flowers. Their porous nature enables excess moisture to evaporate through the sides and toxic salts can escape in the same way. For some plants, however, especially those that need a peat-based compost, plastic pots are sometimes preferred. Because moisture cannot evaporate through these pots it is important not to overwater the plants.

More or less anything that has sides and a base can be used as a planting pot or an ornamental container for plants

in their own pots. Old tea caddies, storage jars and junk-shop finds, teapots and salad bowls, and even wooden boxes can give an original look to a plant display. Plastic containers can be painted in a plain colour and dappled with second and third colours, simple containers can be covered in hessian or printed paper, and baskets can be spray-painted. Blocks of wood can be placed inside a container to raise the height of the plant. Containers made of metal and any material that is not waterproof are best used to hold pots, rather than for direct planting. Place a large plastic box inside, or line with layers of plastic topped with newspaper to absorb excess water draining from the flowerpots.

*Left:* This beautiful terrarium provides an ideal and unusual container for a pretty display of lush plants. *Right:* All sorts of containers can be used to add character to a plant display. This ornate birdcage shows off a *Kalanchoe blossfeldiana* (flaming Katy) in a novel and attractive way, adding an extra dimension to a simple pot plant.

Planting directly into containers not designed for plants demands some thought and much care because of the lack of drainage. The base of the container must be lined with a good layer of clay pellets, which absorb moisture and give good, natural drainage. Charcoal mixed with the potting medium will help to keep it sweet.

## COMPOST

Peat-free composts are becoming increasingly popular as they do not involve the continued destruction of the natural habitat of many plants and animals. The main ingredient in these composts is generally coir, which is obtained from the husk of a coconut and which is a material much used in the past for making ropes and matting.

Gardeners are usually devotees of either peat- or soil-based composts, but it is worth experimenting with a coir-based type. In many ways this will have much the same qualities as peat, such as moisture retention and aeration. Ready-to-use seed and potting composts based on coir are widely available. After use, the compost can be re-used as a mulch around outdoor plants. In future composts formed of materials such as straw, bark and wood fibre may also be available.

Compost provides anchorage for plants and moisture, food and air for roots. Garden soil is unsuitable for houseplants because its quality is variable. It is also badly drained and may contain weed seeds, pests and diseases. Specially prepared composts should be used, therefore, and there are two main types.

Soil-based composts are formed from partially sterilized loam (good topsoil), peat and sharp sand, plus fertilizers. These composts, which are suitable for most houseplants, are heavier than other types and give stability to large plants. In addition, they are unlikely to dry out as fast or so completely as the other types and are richer in minor and trace plant foods than other types of compost.

Most peat-based (and peat-substitute) composts are more uniform in quality than soil-based composts, but they are liable to dry out more rapidly than soil-based types and are difficult to remoisten. They are lighter to carry home by the bag than their soil-based equivalents, but they are poorer in nutrients than soil-based composts (be prepared to feed plants at an earlier stage). They are easily stored even after the bag is opened (just fold over and tie the end), but when these composts are stored in garden centres or nurseries, the peat often becomes compacted. Before using the compost, therefore, shake the bag thoroughly to loosen it.

Left: *Saintpaulia* (African violet) needs to be grown in bright light and where the dainty flowers can be seen in close-up. Dead or damaged leaves should be cut off as soon as they appear, and plants must be watered from the base to keep the leaves dry.

# watering

Without water plants soon die. They also deteriorate when given too much moisture because the compost becomes swamped and airless and roots suffocate and die. The aim of watering is to provide plants with adequate water when they need it. In summer houseplants need more water than in winter, although the compost of winter-flowering houseplants must be kept moist.

## APPLYING WATER

The most popular way to water houseplants is by slowly dribbling water from a watering-can directly on the compost. This is known as 'over the rim' watering. At each application of water, fill the complete area between the compost's surface and the pot's rim. An alternative way is to stand pots in a bowl of water until moisture seeps to the compost's surface. Then, remove the pot and allow excess water to drain away. Air plants, such as tillandsias, should be misted (soaking their leaves in water), while bromeliads that form urns

from rosettes of leaves are mainly watered by filling these 'reservoirs' with water.

## HOLIDAY CARE

Many houseplants are lovingly looked after throughout the year, only to deteriorate or die when you are away on holiday. Both over- and underwatering could kill them, and it is often better to rely on automatic watering devices than on your neighbours.

Leave large plants in their saucers, but put them on a large polythene sheet in a lightly shaded room. During the week before your holiday, water

several times. If the holiday is for only seven to ten days this will usually preserve them.

Small plants can be placed in large trays with 1cm (½in) of water in the base. This will keep them alive for up to a fortnight, if in light shade. Another way is to place a capillary mat on a draining board and to trail one end in a sink filled with water. Alternatively, trail the end in a bowl of water and stand plants on the matting. This system works best for plants in plastic pots filled with peat-based compost and without crocks in the base.

## SAVING A PLANT IN DRY COMPOST

When watering is neglected plants wilt and eventually die. Once a plant is wilting, a point

### A simple wick-waterer

*A simple method of ensuring that your plants get sufficient water while you are away is to support them over a bowl of water and to insert wicks into the compost through the hole in the bottom of the pot and trail the other end in the water.*

## WAYS OF JUDGING WHEN WATER IS NEEDED

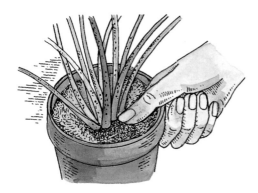

**1** Rubbing a thumb on the surface of compost is a popular way to assess moisture. Only water when the compost is dry and has lost its sponginess.

**3** Moisture-indicator strips (watering signals) can be inserted and left in compost. They change colour when the compost is dry.

**2** Tapping clay pots with a cotton reel attached to a cane is a well-known method: a dull note indicates moist compost, while a ring tells that water is needed.

**4** A moisture meter has a thin, pencil-like probe that is inserted into compost and the moisture level is shown on a dial. It is efficient, but repeated use of the probe will damage roots.

comes when, no matter how much water is given subsequently, it will not recover. However, most plants can be revived if watered soon enough. Stand the pot in a bowl with 3–4cm (1¼–1½in) of water in it. Cut off faded flowers and if the leaves are smooth mist spray them. When moisture rises to the compost's surface, remove the plant and place it in light shade for a few days.

### SAVING A PLANT IN WATERLOGGED COMPOST

If compost becomes totally saturated, air is excluded and roots cease to function. The plant wilts, leaves become limp and slime covers the compost. If noticed early enough plants can be saved. Invert the pot and plant and place a hand under the rootball. Tap the pot's rim on a hard surface so that the rootball slips out. Remove any crocks and

wrap several pieces of kitchen towel around the plant to soak up water. Pick off any root mealy bugs. Leave the rootball wrapped until it is lightly dry. If the rootball is packed with roots, leave it fully exposed to the air. When the surface of the compost is dry but not crumbly, repot the plant into a clean pot, using fresh compost. Leave it for a few days, then water. Do not place it in strong sunlight until it is fully recovered.

*Left*: The yellow pitcher plant *Sarracenia flava* (huntsman's horn) is hardy in temperate climates. This insectivorous plant catches insects but also needs to be given a liquid fertilizer while it is in flower.

# feeding & repotting

Houseplants underachieve if they are not fed regularly once they have filled the pot with roots. Regular feeding is essential if they are to remain healthy and to create an attractive display. Both foliage and summer-flowering houseplants are normally fed at intervals of 10–14 days from early spring to late summer.

Winter-flowering houseplants are fed at the same frequency while they remain in flower.

The most popular way to feed houseplants is by diluting and mixing a concentrated liquid fertilizer in clean tepid water. Adhere to the strength that is recommended by the manufacturer. Before applying the fertilizer, make sure that the compost is moist so that it will be quickly and evenly absorbed. Make up just enough fertilizer to feed your plants on each occasion and do not store any surplus. Keep in one container for fertilizer and do not use it for anything else. Store all chemicals safely.

Using feeding sticks and pills is a clean and quick way to feed houseplants. Feeding sticks are gently pushed into compost, about 1cm (½in) from the pot's side. Pills are also inserted into compost. Some devices enable pills to be inserted without having to dirty your hands on compost. Both feeding sticks and pills provide plants with food over a long period, but they encourage roots to become congested around them.

Do not use feeding sticks and pills after midsummer for plants that flower throughout summer. The fertilizer already released will last for the rest of the flowering season and plants will be able to become dormant after this period. Use feeding sticks or pills on winter-flowering plants in autumn and early winter.

## REPOTTING PLANTS

When a plant needs repotting, use either a combination of plastic pots and peat-based compost, or clay pots and soil-based compost, depending on the plant's requirements. Soak clay pots for 24 hours before using them so that they do not draw water from the compost.

Although pots are available in sizes from 6–38cm (2¼–15in) wide, only five sizes are usually needed: 6cm (2¼in), 8cm (3in), 13cm (5in), 18cm (7in) and 25cm (10in). When repotting, always use only the next size up. Remember, too, always to leave sufficient space between the surface of the compost and the rim of the pot to allow plants to be watered effectively. This space needs to increase in proportion to the pot size: for 6–13cm (2½–5in) wide pots leave 1cm (½in); for 14–19cm (5½–7½in) pots leave 2cm (3/4in); for 20–23cm (8–9in) pots leave 2.5cm (1in); and for 25–30cm (10–12in) pots leave 3.5cm (1¼in).

## Top-dressing

*When a houseplant is in a large pot and cannot be repotted the compost needs to be top-dressed every spring. This involves removing the top 25–36mm (1–1¼in) of old compost and replacing it with fresh. Take care that you not damage the plant's roots when removing the compost. Leave a gap between the top of the compost and the pot's rim so that the plant can be easily watered.*

**1** Water the plant the day before repotting it. Place your fingers over the top of the rootball and invert the pot. Tap the pot's rim on a firm surface. If the rootball resists, run a knife between it and pot to loosen the roots.

**2** Inspect the roots and, when repotting a plant in a clay pot, remove the crock from the rootball's base. Tease out the roots: it may be necessary to use a stiff label or stick.

**3** Select a clean pot, slightly larger than the present one. If repotting into a plastic pot, no crock is needed. However, for a clay pot it is usual to add one.

**4** Place and firm a handful of compost in the pot's base and position the rootball on top. Check that the surface is below the rim, so that the compost can be adequately watered. When the plant is correctly positioned, trickle and gently firm new compost around the old rootball. Do not ram the compost too tightly into the pot.

**5** If necessary, add further compost and gently firm it, leaving the recommended space at the top for watering. Finally, gently tap the side of the pot to level the surface. Then, stand the plant where moisture can drain freely and gently trickle water on top of the compost. Completely fill the watering space. Allow surplus water to drain, later placing the pot in an attractive outer container. Do not water again until the compost shows signs of getting dry – the surface assumes a light colouring.

*Left*: A young plant of *Plumbago capensis* (Cape leadwort) is often trained around a hoop and grown on a windowsill, where its beautiful, phlox-like flowers can be admired throughout summer and into autumn. The plant is vigorous and stems can reach 1.2m (4ft) in length but can be trimmed in spring to keep them shorter.

*Right*: The exotically perfumed *Stephanotis floribunda* (bridal wreath, floradora) thrives if kept in a fairly cool room in winter and protected at all times from draughts and sudden changes in temperature. Young plants look pretty trained around a hoop.

# grooming & care

Unless they are regularly groomed many houseplants become dirty or grow a mass of tangled shoots that dramatically reduce their attractiveness. Dust radically diminishes the ability of leaves to function and create growth. It blocks breathing pores (stomata) and reduces the amount of light reaching growth-activating cells within the leaves.

If large, smooth-surfaced leaves are covered with a thick layer of dirt, use a soft cloth to dust it off lightly before wiping with water. And never place plants in strong sunlight before moisture dries from them: small water droplets act as lenses and intensify the sun's rays, which will burn leaves and cause them to dry and become brown.

Clean, non-chalky soft water is ideal for cleaning leaves; if you live in an area of hard water, use rainwater or tapwater that has been boiled. Although milk, beer and dilute vinegar are also recommended, they do little to shine leaves. Olive-oil is also advocated, but retains dust, which damages leaves. Several proprietary leaf-cleaning substances are available.

## LOOKING AFTER LEAVES
Many plants are grown specifically for their attractive leaves. If these become dirty or

## TRAINING AND SUPPORTING

Climbing plants need support to prevent stems sprawling, becoming tangled and intruding on their neighbours. Split canes and plastic-mesh frameworks are ideal for climbing foliage plants, but *Jasminum polyanthum* (pink jasmine) has more visual appeal when supported with loops of pliable canes or proprietary supports that hook on pots and form a loop 30–38cm (12–15in) high.

**1** When stems are about 30cm (12in) long, insert a pliable cane support into the pot. It should go near to the pot's sides to avoid damaging the roots.

**2** Curl the shoots around the support to create a neat shape.

damaged, this diminishes the display. Cleaning leaves is therefore important and the method for doing this depends on their size and texture. Wipe large, smooth-surfaced leaves with a damp cloth. These include *Ficus elastica* (rubber plant) and *Monstera deliciosa* (Swiss cheese plant). Plants with masses of smooth-surfaced leaves can be inverted and dipped in a bowl of clean water. Some plants have hairy leaves and these are best cleaned carefully using a soft brush.

Damaged leaves can be cut out, together with long and misplaced shoots. When vigorous stems spoil the shape of a plant, use sharp scissors to cut them back to just above a leaf-joint. Azaleas often develop long shoots that are best removed. Cut out dead leaves, but avoid leaving small snags that will die back. If dead leaves are at the top of a shoot, these are best removed by using sharp scissors to cut the stem back to its base.

## DEADHEADING

Most dead flowers on houseplants are picked off individually and placed on a compost heap. Azaleas produce a profusion of flowers over several weeks; as the first ones fade, hold the shoot and carefully pinch them off. When you are deadheading cyclamen, pull off each faded flower together with its stem. Hold the stem firmly and give it a sharp tug. It will separate from the plant's base. If just the flower is removed, the stem slowly decays and encourages other flowers and stems to decay. It also looks unsightly. Place the flowers and stems on a compost heap; do not leave them at the plant's base.

# 2 FLOWERING POT PLANTS

Flowering pot plants will generally be less permanent than other indoor plants, either because they are difficult or impossible to keep going once they have flowered or because the plants are not particularly attractive while they are 'resting' in preparation for the next flowering period.

A large number of plants have been developed and introduced commercially in recent years to provide colour for a limited period, and there is now such a wide choice available that it is possible to have something in flower practically all year round. Cyclamens and azaleas, for example, flower in winter or early spring, while scented spring primroses, celosias and calceolarias bloom in summer. Some plants, however, such as chrysanthemums, can be bought in flower all year.

These plants make a colourful, and sometimes fragrant, contribution when they are in flower, but they should be regarded as short-term additions to the indoor scene. They are usually planted in the garden or even thrown away once the flowering period is over. Some

are annuals and so last only one season anyway; others are short-lived perennials, or perennials that have been reared in special conditions or sometimes artificially treated so that they come into flower at an unusual time or retain what is, in fact, an unnatural dwarf habit.

Feeding the plants generously and removing dead and dying flowers should help to extend the flowering period. Most pot plants need good light, but check each plant's own care requirements carefully. Try to protect plants from sudden changes in temperature and from draughts in winter, and remember that many winter-flowering plants need temperatures that are a little lower than those of most living rooms.

A healthy pot plant makes a good centrepiece for a table or

*Left*: Flowering pot plants are ideal for creating seasonal displays. Once flowering is over, plants can be removed and the next group brought indoors. *Above:* Azaleas and pot chrysanthemums mingle with orchids in this cool conservatory. Complementary containers and surfaces at different heights help to enrich the display.

windowsill, and a brightly coloured flowering plant placed in its pot among foliage plants and ferns will bring the arrangement to life. A visit to your garden centre at any time of year will give you a wide choice of pot plants in flower, and many supermarkets now have a good selection.

# plant directory

### Achimines hybrids (hot-water plant, cupid's bower)

Much grown by Victorians, these plants have masses of slightly fragrant, flaring trumpet-shaped flowers from spring to autumn. Many colourful hybrids, including some with variegated leaves, have been introduced, and the flowers may be purple, mauve, red, white or blue. Plants are easily grown afresh each year from rhizomes.

Achimenes need a position in bright light with shade from full sun. They tolerate normal room temperatures. Water frequently with tepid water and feed once a week.

### Astilbe arendsii (plume of feathers)

More often seen in the garden, astilbes make attractive indoor plants for spring and early summer. The flower plumes are usually in shades pink, but red and white cultivars can be found.

In the house astilbes need fairly bright light with shade from full sun and normal room temperatures. Provide high humidity and water well. After flowering, plant in a damp, semi-shaded part of the garden.

### Azalea
See **Rhododendron**

### Begonia

This is a large genus, containing plants that are grown for their foliage as well as for their flowers. Tuberous begonia hybrids, B. x tuberhybrida, with their beautiful, mainly double, rose-like flowers, make lovely flowering pot plants for the summer months, and the group also includes Multiflora and Pendula begonias. Multiflora begonias have many small, single or double flowers. Pendula begonias have similar small flowers and rather arching stems, making them good plants for hanging baskets.

Winter-flowering begonias are low-growing evergreen plants, with

*Far left:* Many colourful hybrids of *Achimenes* (hot water plant) have been introduced in recent years.
*Above left: Calceolaria* plants make bright spring- and summer-flowering perennials.
*Below left:* Flowering pot plants like *Cyclamen persicum* do not often survive more than one season as houseplants.
*Right:* Hydrangeas create superb displays of colour from late spring to early summer.

masses of single, semi-double or double flowers from late autumn to early spring, such as the justly popular *B.* 'Gloire de Lorraine', with its masses of small pink flowers in winter, and the many Elatior hybrids.

Begonias need bright but indirect light. Keep them in normal summer room temperatures, with spring warmth to bring them into growth, and make sure that the potting compost is evenly moist.

### *Calceolaria* Herbeohybrida Group (slipper flower, pouch flower, pocketbook plant)

These bushy biennials have distinctive puffed flowers, which give the plant its common names. Buy plants in bud and keep them in a bright, sunny but cool place, with a top temperature of 16°C (61°C), for late spring or early summer yellow, orange or red flowers, which last a month or more.

### *Celosia argentea* var. *cristata* Plumosa Group (cockscomb)

This upright perennial, usually grown as an annual, can be a bedding plant, but its colourful of flowers make it popular indoors. Grow in a light, well-ventilated room out of direct sun at normal room temperatures. Feed once a fortnight and discard after flowering.

### *Chrysanthemum* cvs.

Pot chrysanthemums are now available throughout the year, and they remain in flower for more than a month. When the display ends they are best discarded, although they can be planted out in a sunny border. They need bright light (but not full sun) in a fairly cool room. Keep the compost moist but not waterlogged.

### *Cyclamen persicum*

Also sold as *C. latifolium*, this popular tuberous perennial has beautifully marbled, heart-shaped leaves and pink, red or white flowers from early winter to spring. Grow in bright but filtered light with a temperature of 13–16°C (55–61°F). Place plants out of draughts. They need moderately warm, humid air. Reduce watering after flowering and keep dry during dormancy. Start to water and feed again when new growth appears.

### *Erica* (heather)

Two species make excellent winter-flowering pot plants, *E. gracilis* (Cape heath) and *E.* x *hiemnalis*, but they must be kept in cool rooms and watered with soft water. Both have masses of tubular flowers, which are tiny and pink or rosy-purple on *E. gracilis*, and larger and pink with white tips on *E.* x *hiemnalis*.

These ericas need lime-free, constantly moist compost and good light. They will tolerate temperatures of 4–13°C (40–55°F).

### *Exacum affine* (Persian violet)

This compact, pretty plant has small, fragrant, mauve flowers with bright yellow centres and heart-shaped leaves. It looks good on a coffee table or bedroom windowsill where it will be in good bright light but not strong sun. It will grow in normal room temperatures with fresh air in hot weather. Water generously and keep the humidity high. Pinch out dying flowers and feed every ten days to ensure that you have flowers all summer long.

### *Hydrangea macrophylla*

Pot hydrangeas are available in flower from spring to autumn, and they can be planted out in the garden once they have flowered. The mopheads of flowers are available in white and shades of pale pink and blue. Hydrangeas do best in cool conditions, in temperatures no higher than 20°C (68°F), in good but indirect light. Water well when plants are in flower and feed once a week.

**Pericallis x hybrida (cineraria)**
Also known as *Cineraria cruentus*,
*C.* x *hybrida*, *Senecio cruentus* and
*S.* x *hybridus*, these colourful
perennials are probably best known
as cinerarias. From winter to spring
they produce daisy-like flowers in
bright shades of blue, pink, red and
orange. Despite being popular gift
plants, they are quite difficult to
please. The compost must be kept
moist but must also drain freely, and
the plants should not be exposed to
either draughts or high temperatures.
They like indirect light and an even
room temperature, which must never
be higher than 15°C (60°F).

The plants are usually available
in late winter and spring and will
flower for up to two months. Feed
them once a fortnight and deadhead
regularly to encourage new buds
to form. Discard plants after flowering
is finished.

**Primula**
The genus includes a number of
different species that can be treated
as indoor plants. *P. malacoides*

(fairy primrose, baby primrose) is a
dainty, short-lived plant, which flowers
in winter and has a slight but lovely
fragrance. It can sometimes be
persuaded to flower for a second
season if it is kept well. The typical
primrose flowers, in a range of
pale purples, pinks and white, are
carried in whorls on tall, straight
stems, growing from rosettes of
tooth-edged leaves.

*P. obconia* (German primrose,
poison primrose) has larger flowers,
which may be red, pink, blue or
white. Contact with the foliage
can cause painful allergic rashes
in people with sensitive skin, and
the leaves are poisonous so
handle it only with care.

The flowers of *P. sinensis* (Chinese
primrose) have frilly-edged petals and
are available in shades of red and
orange as well as a muted blue-pink.

Primulas need bright, indirect light
and a fairly cool temperature of
10–13°C (50–55°F). Water them
generously and maintain a high
level of humidity. Feed every two
to three weeks.

*Top: Sinningia speciosa*
(gloxinia) has characteristic
brightly coloured and
bordered petals and large
velvety leaves.
*Above:* A healthy *Pericallis* x
*hybrida* will keep its flowers
longer if it is regularly fed
and misted. It should not be
given too much heat.

*Above:* A single pot-grown azalea, *Rhododendron* cv., can form a centrepiece for a table or windowsill.
*Right*: Several tender primula species can be grown indoors for winter flowers. *Primula obconica* (poison primrose) has the largest flowers and these have a lovely fragrance.

## Rhododendron

The large genus contains the well-known evergreen garden shrubs but also the group of small to medium-sized plants that are known as azaleas and that produce a mass of flowers in white or shades of yellow, orange, pink and red. Azaleas may be deciduous and evergreen, and there are numerous subdivisions within each group. The evergreen Indica (Indian) hybrids are widely bought for their large, funnel-shaped flowers, which are borne in winter. Azaleas must have ericaceous compost, which should be kept just moist in winter. They need bright but indirect light and high humidity. Keep them in a cool place, with a maximum temperature of 13–16°C (55–61°F), when they are in flower. In summer, after they have flowered, keep them in a shaded, cool place outdoors. Bring them indoors again in the early winter before the first frosts and being to water again as flowerbuds appear.

## Sinningia speciosa (gloxinia)

Increasingly exotic-looking hybrids of this plant have been bred in recent years. The rosettes of leaves are soft and velvety, and the large, flaring bell-shaped to tubular flowers, in white or shades of red and violet-blue, often have contrasting throats and may be bordered in white or contrasting colours. Gloxinias need bright, indirect light and a warm temperature, 20–22°C (68–72°F), day and night in summer (when they are in flower). Keep the air humid by standing the pots on a tray of moist pebbles but do not spray the leaves or flowers and water plants from below. Feed once a fortnight in the growing season.

# 3 FLOWERING HOUSEPLANTS

A well-cared for plant that has 'lived' in a house for several years and that still flowers duly in its season is as much a source of pleasure – and pride – as a well-polished antique. These are the flowering houseplants, as opposed to the flowering pot plants, which come and go and are often dispensed with at the end of the flowering season. Many flowering houseplants can become quite large and will eventually need to be given plenty of room, perhaps in a hall with a high ceiling or standing by a patio door, or even in a conservatory or sun room.

*Left:* Grouping houseplants of similar sizes or textures enhances their beauty. Here, the delicate flowers of *Saintpaulia ionnantha* (African violets) are echoed by the leaves of *Adiantum raddianum* (maidenhair fern).
*Right:* The bright yellow flowerheads of *Pachystachys lutea* (lollipop plant) are formed by a cone of overlapping bracts. It flowers from late spring to early autumn and grows well in a room that is cool in summer.
*Below right: Euphorbia pulcherrima* (poinsettia) has become a classic midwinter plant. The showy bracts make a cheerful seasonal display. Most poinsettias have deep crimson bracts, but white, pink and scarlet cultivars are available.

To stand the test of time, a plant must be well chosen in the first place. There is no point in being seduced by a light-craving hot-house plant if you live in a dark, cool cottage, just as, if your fifth-floor flat gets the full glare of the midday sun, there is little point in buying a plant that needs a position in shade. Choose from the justly popular, well-established favourites that are widely available, or search out something a little different from a specialist grower.

Buy from a reputable supplier. Look out for a healthy-looking specimen that is not pot bound. It should have plenty of new buds and exhibit vigorous, but not soft, growth.

Your plant will need to be repotted, into a pot one size larger, as its roots fill its pot, and this should done at the end of the dormant period. This may have to be done every year, especially while the plant is young and growing quickly. Once the plant has exhausted the minerals in the compost – after approximately six to eight weeks – feed it with proprietary fertilizer during the growing period.

*Left*: Anthurium scherzerianum (flamingo flower) has bold foliage as well as striking red flowers in spring and summer.
*Above*: Aphelandra squarrosa will lose its magnificent leaves very quickly if its roots dry out.
*Right*: Bougainvillea (paper flower) makes a spectacular deciduous indoor climber for a warm, light, sunny position.

# plant directory

### Acalypha hispida (chenille plant)

An old favourite, this is grown for its softly drooping tassels or catkins, which hang from the stems from midsummer to mid-autumn and give rise to another common name: red-hot cat's tail. These tassels are made up of hundreds of minute flowers, which are usually deep scarlet, although there are forms with cream and greenish tassels. The plant grows to a height of 1–1.2m (3–4ft) with a spread of 30–45cm (12–14in). Stand in bright, indirect light with a normal room temperature in summer but no lower than 15°C (59°F) in winter. Water freely in summer and keep the compost moist in winter. Feed every 10–14 days from spring to autumn.

### Aeschynanthus radicans (lipstick vine)

Also sold as *A. lobbianus* and *A. radicans* var. *lobbianus*, this is a trailing perennial, with cascades of little fleshy leaves and tubular red flowers with cream throats. The stems grow to 45–60cm (18–24in) long, and this is an ideal plant for a hanging basket in a sun room or conservatory. It needs bright light, but avoid a position in full sun in summer, and a warm summer temperature. In winter it should be cooler, with a minimum of 13°C (55°F). Water with tepid water, freely in summer, more sparingly in winter, and feed monthly from late spring and throughout the summer. Mist regularly to maintain a humidity.

### Allamanda

*A. cathartica* (golden trumpet) is a vigorous climber with large yellow flowers from summer to autumn and glossy, dark green leaves. Support the stems. *A. schottii* (syn. *A. neriifolia*) is shrubbier, bearing golden-yellow flowers from spring to autumn. Both need good light and indirect sun, with minimum winter temperatures of 18°C (65°F). Water freely in the growing season, feeding every 2–3 weeks. In winter keep the compost just moist.

### Anthurium (flamingo flower, tail flower)

*A. scherzerianum* is a terrestrial or epiphytic perennial with red, palette-shaped spathes, each of which has a

curly, wick-like spire of tiny flowers, from spring to autumn. It is a compact plant, 30cm (12in) high and 30–38cm (12–15in) across, and has attractive, lance-shaped leaves. Similar, but larger – up to 45cm (18in) high and 30cm (12in) across – is *A. andreanum* (painter's palette, oilcloth flower), which has a straight 'tail' and red spathes. There are cultivars with pink, yellow and orange spathes.

Anthuriums need bright but indirect light and normal room temperatures in summer but no lower than 15–18°C (59–64°F) in winter. Water generously in summer but keep the compost just moist in winter. Keep the surrounding air moist and feed every 10–14 days from mid-spring to early autumn.

### Aphelandra squarrosa (saffron spike, zebra plant)

This compact shrub is grown for its boldly patterned foliage as well as for the pineapple-like yellow bracts, which form the showy part of its flowerheads. The cultivar 'Louisae' has prominent white ribs on the leaves, and the golden-yellow flower spikes are streaked with red. Plants grow to about 75cm (30in) high and to about 40cm (16in) wide. They need bright, indirect light and normal room temperatures in summer but a winter minimum of 12–15°C (54–59°F). Water generously in summer and moderately in winter. Feed every 10–14 days. Cut off flowerheads when they die and cut the plant back to keep it bushy if necessary.

### Begonia

In addition to the many cultivars of tuberous begonias grown for their beautiful flowers, the genus contains several other worthwhile species. *B. scharffii* (syn. *B. haageana*; elephant ear begonia) is a shrub-like begonia with large, curiously shaped leaves, which make the plant interesting all year round. The pale pink summer flowers are a bonus. It will grow to 1.2m (4ft) high with a spread of 60cm (2ft). *B. metallica* (metallic leaf begonia) is best known as a foliage plant, but it, too, has pretty white flowers, borne in clusters in late summer. It grows to about 1m (3ft) high and 60cm (2ft) across.

Both plants need bright but indirect light, with some direct sun in winter. Normal room temperatures are acceptable in summer, but a constant temperature of 13–15°C (55–60°F) is needed in winter. Too much summer heat can be fatal. Keep the atmosphere humid, especially during the summer. Water the plants moderately in summer but only sparingly in winter. Feed every 14 days in summer.

### Bougainvillea glabra

A young bougainvillea is a wonderfully showy plant for a sunny windowsill, but it is a scrambler that will need to be trained and given ample space as it grows. The papery, purple 'flowers' are really bracts and grow in clusters through the summer. Bougainvilleas must have ample, bright light all year round. They need to be warm in summer, but with cooler temperatures, 7–12°C (45–54°F), in winter. Water sparingly in summer and keep the compost almost dry in winter. The plants are best grown best in a conservatory when they are more than three years old.

not too hot, in summer, with a temperature of 15–19°C (59–66°F), but cooler, 4–10°C (39–50°F), in winter. Keep the compost moist and feed every seven to ten days in summer. Cut back all the stems after flowering and let the plant rest, watering sparingly, in winter.

### Cestrum nocturnum (night jessamine)

Similar to jasmine, with an equally strong and beautiful scent. When young this night-flowering plant is ideal for a light living room, but it can grow to 3m (10ft) and then needs a conservatory or large, light space. Train the twining stems up canes and along wires. Position in bright light, but with protection from full summer sun. Plants need a minimum winter temperature of 7°C (45°F). Water generously in summer and moderately in winter.

### Columnea (goldfish plant)

There are several popular columneas and all are trailing plants for sun rooms and conservatories. They are useful as they flower throughout winter, from autumn to early spring. *C. microphylla* trails to 1.8m (6ft) and has bright orange-red flowers and hairy leaves. The flowers of *C.* x *banksii* are similar but have orange markings, the dark green leaves are glossy, and the stems are a more modest 1m (3ft). *C. gloriosa* has stems to 1.2m (4ft) long; it bears scarlet flowers with a yellow patch, and has

### Brunfelsia pauciflora (yesterday, today and tomorrow)

This shrubby plant, formerly known as *B. calycina* (syn. *B. eximia*), has pretty flowers that change colour from violet to white as they age. It flowers all summer when growing well and will get to 60cm (2ft) high and 30cm (12in) across. Position plants in bright, indirect light and keep warm in summer, but not above 21°C (70°F); in winter they need a constant temperature of 10–13°C (50–55°F). Water generously and mist the leaves in summer, feeding once a month when plants are in flower. Water sparingly during the dormant period.

### Calathea crocata

Most members of the genus are grown as foliage plants (see page 47), but this species produces yellow flowers, resembling small orchids, on erect stems above the leaves. Plants grow to about 30cm (12in) high and 23cm (9in) across. They need bright but indirect light and high humidity. A year-round temperature of 15–21°C (60–70°F) is ideal. Make sure plants are sited out of draughts. Water freely during the growing season and feed every 14 days, but in winter just keep the compost moist.

### Campanula isophylla (falling stars, Italian bellflower)

This is a low-growing plant, to 15cm (6in) high, with a spread of 30–45cm (12–18in). The lovely pale blue or white, bell-shaped flowers are borne throughout summer. Its trailing habit makes it ideal for a tall pot or stand or for a hanging basket. Position in good, indirect light. It needs to be warm, but pale green hairy leaves. *C. gloriosa* 'Purpurea' has purple leaves. *C. hirta* is one of the smaller species: the strong, creeping stems bear a mass of red flowers in spring.

Grow columneas in bright light but out of direct sun. They need normal summer temperatures and a winter temperature of about 16°C (61°F), but no lower than 13°C (55°F). They need humid conditions, and the compost must be kept moist at all times. Feed weekly once the flower buds appear.

### *Cuphea ignea* (cigar flower)

Formerly known as *C. platycentra*, this compact shrub produces long, tubular, bright red flowers, which are tipped with dark purple and ash white, from spring until the beginning of winter or even longer. *C. ignea* 'Alba' has white flowers, and 'Variegata' has yellow-marked leaves. Cupheas need bright light but with some shade from full sun in summer. They will grow in normal summer temperatures but need a cooler temperature, 10–13°C (50–55°F), during the winter rest. Cupheas can be stood outside in warm summer weather as long as good humidity can be maintained. Water generously in spring and summer and feed every two weeks. Water sparingly in winter and do not feed.

### *Episcia* (carpet plant, flame violet)

A close relation of *Saintpaulia* (African violet), episcias are flowering houseplants grown also for their foliage. The variable *E. cupreata* has flame red flowers and quilted leaves. *E. dianthiflora* (syn. *Alsobia dianthiflora*; lace flower) has plump, downy leaves and white flowers with fringed petals, similar to those of *Dianthus* (garden pinks). Both species grow to only about 8cm (3in) high. They have trailing stems or runners to 30cm (12in) long, from which new plants can be grown. Position the plants in good light, avoiding strong sun. Normal room temperatures are suitable for summer, but plants need a winter minimum of 13°C (55°F). Try to give plants a slight drop in temperature each evening and make sure that the air around them is humid by misting and standing their pots in a dish of wet pebbles.

### Euphorbia (spurge)

This is a large genus, containing plants that can be grown in the open garden as well as several that are normally grown as houseplants. *E. milii* (crown of thorns) is a handsome plant, grown for the colourful, showy bracts – red, yellow or white – that surround the tiny, insignificant flowers, which are borne in spring and early summer and almost non-stop in a really bright light. It has rather sprawling stems with prominent spines and grows to a height of 1m (3ft). This euphorbia is a popular, undemanding plant as long as you can find a sunny spot for it. It needs a bright position, but shaded from midday summer sun. In summer it will grow in normal room temperatures, but it needs a winter minimum of 13°C (55°F). Water sparingly and feed once a month.

*E. pucherrima* (poinsettia, Mexican flame leaf) is often available for Christmas decorations, and the bright red bracts are certainly eye-catching and cheerful. It is sometimes treated as an annual and thrown away in spring, because it needs a period of rest, in a cool, shaded position, with two months in darkness for half each day, in summer, which can be difficult to provide in most people's homes. Stop watering after flowering and only begin again when new growth begins.

### Gardenia augusta (Cape jasmine)

Also known as *G. florida*, *G. grandiflora* and *G. jasminoides*, these shrubs bear beautiful, fragrant flowers from summer to autumn. Plants grow to 12m (40ft) high in the wild, but when they are grown in pots, heights of 60cm (2ft) are more usual. Grow in good but filtered light. Plants need ericaceous compost. Water freely in summer, using soft water, and feed every month. In winter plants need a minimum temperature of 10°C (50°F).

### Hibiscus rosa-sinensis (rose of China)

This is another good plant for a sunny position. Most often seen with deep reddish-pink flowers, it can also have yellow, orange, pale pink or white blooms. The cultivar 'Cooperi' has cream- and pink-variegated leaves. Orange-flowered cultivars include 'Tivoli' and 'Royal Orange'. The large flowers are short-lived, but new buds open regularly through summer. A well-cared for hibiscus can live for many years and grow to 1.5m (5ft) high if not cut back. Grow hibiscus in good light with an even temperature of 18°C (64°F) or above all year round to give non-stop flowering. If you want to give the plant a winter rest, the temperature should be 10–15°C (50–60°F). Water plants fairly generously and feed once a week while they are in flower. In winter water moderately and do not feed if you going to allow the plant a dormant period. Hibiscus, which are native to China, are long-lived plants, but are all too often lost through poor treatment when grown as houseplants. Underwatering causes buds to drop and leaves to fall; underfeeding reduces flowering; low humidity, draughts, sudden temperature changes and over-generous watering are also damaging.

### Hoya (wax flower)

*H. carnosa* (wax plant), which bears clusters of waxy, scented flowers, looks and smells exotic, but it is not too difficult to grow. Its climbing stems will grow up to 4.5m (15ft) and must be trained up canes or trellis or along wires. It looks natural and attractive trained up a moss pole. Position in bright light, with some shade from strong summer sun. It needs a summer minimum temperature of 16°C (61°F), and in winter it needs to be kept at around 10°C (50°F) and not below 7°C (45°F). Give the plant fresh air in summer, but keep the humidity high.

Another popular hoya is *H. lanceolata* subsp. *bella* (syn. *H. bella*; miniature wax plant), which grows to about 45cm (18in) high and across, and it is perfect for a hanging basket. It needs more warmth in winter, 13°C (55°F), and must be well protected from strong summer sun.

### Ixora coccinea (flame of the woods)

This eye-catching plant needs some care. Its big flowerheads are clustered with little red, white, yellow or pink flowers, and it forms an evergreen, bushy plant, which can grow up to 38cm (15in) in a year. It needs bright, filtered light, away from direct sun. Water and mist spray plants regularly, using tepid, boiled water, but after flowering water only sparingly and rest the plant for about two months. Do not repot these plants unless it becomes absolutely necessary, when an ericaceous compost should be used.

*Far left: Euphorbia milii* (crown of thorns) is grown for the waxy bracts around its tiny yellow flowers. *Left:* The pinkish-white flowers of *Justicia brandegeeana* (shrimp plant) project from overlapping bracts. Grown in good sun, the plant is covered with flowers from spring to autumn. *Right: Passiflora incarnata* (maypops) a strongly growing passionflower, which has beautifully scented flowers in summer, is native to North America.

## Jasminum polyanthum (pink jasmine)

The lovely pink jasmine, with its pink buds and clusters of scented white flowers, is fairly easy to grow and flowers indoors in winter. A climber, which can reach 3m (10ft), it is generally restricted and trained over a hoop by wrapping the tendrils around the support. Cut it back after flowering. Grow in bright light. It does best in cooler rooms, heated to 7–10°C (45–50°F) in winter.

## Justicia brandegeeana (shrimp plant)

Formerly known as *Beloperone guttata* (syn. *Drejerella guttata, J. guttata*), this evergreen shrub is a charming curiosity. The flowerheads consist of shrimp-like bracts, terminating in a white, tubular flower. It makes a small plant, 30–40cm (12–16in) high and across, and is easy to grow, provided you are able to give it a sunny windowsill. Although it needs bright sunlight it will do best with some protection from direct summer sun. In summer grow in normal, warm room temperatures. In winter it needs cooler temperatures, 10–16°C (50–61°F), and will tolerate temperatures as low as 7°C (45°F). Water generously in summer and sparingly in winter. Grow two or three plants together for a good show, and cut them back in spring if they begin to get 'leggy'.

## Mandevilla

*M. sanderi* 'Rosea' (syn. *Dipladenia sanderi* 'Rosea') is a gorgeous and versatile plant. Its large pink flowers appear in profusion throughout the summer if the air is kept warm and humid, and it can be trained as a climber, to 4.5m (15ft) or pruned as a shrub. *M. laxa* (syn. *Dipladenia laxa, M. suaveolens*: Chilean jasmine) has white, extremely fragrant flowers. Mandevillas need good light but with protection from strong sun. Try to maintain a constant temperature of about 21°C (70°F) in summer and 15°C (60°F) in winter, with a minimum of 13°C (55°F). Water generously in summer and fairly sparingly in winter. Feed flowering plants once a week.

## Manettia luteorubra (Brazilian firecracker)

Formerly known as *M. bicolor* and *M. inflata*, this is a fast-growing, undemanding and attractive plant. It grows well in normal room conditions and flowers almost all year round. Long, red, downy tubular flowers, tipped with yellow, peep out from glossy, deep green leaves. Stems grow rapidly and can reach 3m (10ft). Grow in full sun with a minimum winter temperature of 7°C (45°F). Keep the compost moist at all times, and water more generously in spring and summer. Train the plant up a pyramid of canes, tying in the new shoots as they grow.

## Pachystachys lutea (lollipop plant)

A bright and fairly adaptable plant, about 50cm (20in) high, this bears bold, clear, yellow flowerheads made up of overlapping bracts with little, white projecting flowers from spring to autumn. It needs good bright light, but not full sun. Give it normal room temperatures throughout the year, with a winter minimum of 13°C (55°F). Water generously when the plant is in flower but quite sparingly in winter. Keep the surrounding air moist in warm weather. Repot and trim back every spring.

## Passiflora caerulea (common passionflower)

Also known as blue passionflower and passion vine, the large and complex summer flowers of this lovely climber can be followed by orange fruits. Although passionflowers can be grown in protected gardens, they are not reliably hardy. Indoors, grow in bright sunlight. They need normal summer temperatures, but should be allowed a winter rest at about 10°C (50°F). Water plants extremely generously while they are flower, but keep the compost just moist in winter. A young plant can be trained around a hoop, but it is vigorous and does justice to a trellis as it grows. Too much feeding can encourage the plant to produce more leaves than flowers.

*Left: Pelargonium* 'Parasol' is typical of the regal type with its many-petalled flowers splashed in pink and white and streaked with deep red markings.

### Pelargonium (geranium)

This old favourite is at home everywhere. There are three main types grown for their flowers: zonal pelargoniums, which often have bold zones of contrasting colour on the leaves; regal pelargoniums, which have bigger, fancier flowers and irregularly edged leaves; and ivy-leaved or trailing pelargoniums, which have lobed, rather fleshy leaves. If you provide plenty of sun and make sure that plants are kept reasonably warm in winter, they will flower cheerfully all year round, but they can be given a cooler winter rest. The bushy types can be quite compact or can reach 60cm (24in) high with a spread of 25–45cm (10–18in). *P. peltatum* (trailing geranium) has shiny, ivy-like leaves. These plants are perfect for hanging baskets or as part of a display on a light, open landing or indoor balcony. They trail for up to 1m (3ft). Pelargoniums, especially zonal and regal types, need full sun. They will survive at normal room temperature all year round, with a winter minimum of 7–10°C (45–50°F). Water fairly generously and feed every two to three weeks when in flower. If plants are resting in lower temperatures keep the compost barely moist. Bushy types become 'leggy' in inadequate light.

### Plumbago auriculata (Cape leadwort)

Formerly known as *P. capensis*, this unattractively named plant has the most attractive blue flowers. It can be allowed to trail but is best trained to a support. Like *Passiflora caerulea*, it is fairly tolerant but must have a cool winter rest. Grow in fairly bright light, but not full midday sun, with normal summer temperatures. The winter temperature should be 7–10°C (45–50°F). Water generously when in flower in summer and autumn, sparingly in winter.

### Saintpaulia cvs. (African violet)

African violets are one of the most familiar of houseplants, thanks partly to central heating and partly to the ease with which new plants can be propagated from the velvety leaves. These pretty little plants can be kept in flower all year but they can be quite fussy. They usually grow to 8–10cm (3–4in) high and 15–23cm (6–9in) across, but tiny, and exquisite, miniature forms are now becoming popular. African violets look well in groups, and this helps to keep the humidity high, which is essential, as are acid compost and regular feeding. Grow in good, bright light but avoid strong sun. They need steady warmth all year round with a minimum temperature of 15°C (60°F).

### Spathiphyllum wallisii (peace lily)

An elegant, rhizomatous plant, this has long, gleaming leaves and tall flowers, consisting of a white, sail-like spathe surrounding a creamy-white flower spike. The flowers are borne from late spring throughout summer. Plants needs warmth, with minimum winter temperatures of 10°C (50°F), and humidity. In summer they should be shaded from strong, direct sun, but in winter need a bright position.

They hate draughts. Feed every ten days throughout the year, but with the fertilizer at half strength in winter.

### Stephanotis floribunda (bridal wreath, floradora)

Formerly known as *S. jasminoides*, this lovely and desirable plant has glossy, leathery leaves and headily scented, waxy flowers from early summer to mid-autumn. Stephanotis will climb and spread to 3m (10ft) or so and needs to be trained to a trellis or along wires. Grow in good light with shade from full sun in summer; plants need full light in winter. provide a constant temperatures of about 18–21°C (64–70°F) in summer and a winter minimum of 13°C (55°F). While plants are in flower water generously and provide high humidity, especially when temperatures are high, and feed once every two weeks. Water sparingly in winter.

### Streptocarpus cvs. (Cape primrose, Cape cowslip)

Many colourful cultivars have been developed, and there is a wide choice of white-, pink-, mauve-, blue- or purple-flowered plants. The common name seems a misnomer, for the flowers, borne on long, upright stems, resemble single foxgloves or large violets, growing from a loose rosette of rounded leaves. Grow in good, indirect light, with a temperature up to 15°C (60°F) in summer and a steady 10–13°C (50–55°F) in winter. Water freely in summer and stand plants on a tray of wet pebbles to increase humidity. Water more sparingly in winter. Do not mist.

# insectivorous plants

Insectivorous plants are of three main types: pitcher plants, sticky-leaved plants and fly traps. They are interesting rather than lovely, but they are not easy to keep in cultivation, requiring both a protected environment and high levels of humidity.

Some types of insectivorous plants, such as the sarracenias, produce enzymes to digest trapped insects. Larger species may also attract larger animals, such as frogs, mice or even small birds.

## plant directory

**Darlingtonia californica (pitcher plant, cobra lily)**
This rosette-forming perennial plant from northern California and Oregon looks just like a cluster of snakes. The nectar attracts insects, which become trapped in the plant's greenish-yellow 'pitcher'. It needs good, indirect light, normal summer temperatures and a cooler winter temperature of 7–10°C (45–50°F). These plant need high humidity and generous watering, especially in summer.

**Dionaea muscipula (Venus fly-trap)**
This is, perhaps, the best known of the insectivorous plants. It is native to North and South Carolina and can be grown in a conservatory. Plants form rosettes of yellow-green leaves, which are composed of two hinged lobes. Each leaf is edged with spines. When an insect touches a spine, the leaf closes around it. Plants grow to about 45cm (18in) high and to 15cm (6in) across. Grow in good but filtered light and stand the pots in saucers of water to keep the compost moist.

**Drosera (sundew, daily dew)**
This is a large genus, but only a few species are available. *D. binata*, an evergreen perennial, has long-stalked, deeply cut leaves, which are covered with red-stalked hairs. They secrete a sticky fluid, which insects mistake for nectar and adhere to. *D. capensis* (Cape sundew) grows about 30cm (12in) high and to 15cm (6in) across. The spoon-shaped leaves are covered with red or green hairs. Rose-pink flowers are borne from spring to autumn and sometimes winter. Plants should be grown in a mix of equal parts sand and peat or peat substitute. Grow in full light, shaded from hot, direct sun. They need a minimum temperature of 2°C (36°F).

**Nepenthes x coccinea (monkey cup, pitcher plant)**
This hybrid has broad, arching leaves with 'pitchers', to 15cm (6in) long, hanging from the tips. The pitchers are yellow-green and are mottled with purplish-red. Plants, which can grow to 6m (20ft) but are unlikely to achieve this in cultivation, are good for hanging baskets. Grow in good but filtered light, with protection from direct sun. They need a minimum daytime temperature of 24°C (75°F); the summer night-time temperature should be 21°C (70°F) and the summer night temperature should be 15°C (60°F).

*Above*: The deep, horn-shaped pitchers of *Sarracenia leucophylla* are veined in purple and decoratively frilled caps. It is very tall – about 75cm (30in) high.

**Sarracenia (pitcher plant)**
The genus contains several pitcher plants that can be grown in cold or cool greenhouses or even on a sunny windowsill. *S. purpurea* (huntsman's cup) has purple or green pitchers, veined with purple. *S. flava* (yellow trumpet, huntsman's horn) has slender, trumpet-like pitchers, which can reach almost 1m (3ft), although they are likely to be shorter in cultivation. *S. x catesbaei* has green to dark purple pitchers to 75cm (30in).

# 4 FOLIAGE PLANTS

Plants grown mainly for their leaves often form the backbone of a houseplant collection. Many foliage plants are extremely undemanding and long lived. They can grow to a good size or form the most pleasing shapes, and they can take up a permanent place in the home.

A mature, large foliage plant, such as the ever-popular *Ficus elastica* (rubber plant) or *Ficus benjamina* (weeping fig), can be at its best displayed alone as a specimen plant, standing in a large, handsome container on the floor. Smaller, but equally distinctive, foliage plants provide perfect specimen plants for tables, sideboards and cupboard tops and for broad windowsills and shelves. These include some adaptable plants such as *Araucaria heterophylla* (Norfolk Island Pine). Foliage plants that creep or trail can be shown off in indoor hanging baskets or trailing down from pots placed on high shelves, and almost any green-leaved foliage plant will act as a foil to a flowering plant. Most rooms in the house have a niche for a foliage plant, and they can be excellent in circulation spaces such as halls and landings where ceilings are often high.

Favourites, such as *Monstera deliciosa* (Swiss cheese plant), *Ficus benjamina*, *Schefflera elegantissima* (false aralia), yucca and palm, can grow to well over 1m (3ft) high. Growth may be slow, but eventually you will need a room with a high ceiling. Large entrance halls and landings and half-landings on the stairs can be good places for them as they mature but living rooms are generally ideal in their young days.

Like smaller plants, the large foliage plants can group extremely well when they are young, with their contrasting leaf shapes setting each other off to great advantage. For this sort of arrangement a raised trough works well and gives the plants the height they need at this stage of their lives.

*Opposite*: Many cultivars of dieffenbachia are grown for their magnificent leaves, spotted and streaked in green, cream and white.
*Below*: The archetypal plant of the 1970s, *Chlorophytum comosum* (spider plant) is becoming popular once again.

# trailing & cascading plants

Foliage plants that trail or cascade can be shown off to the full in hanging bowls or baskets or trailing down from pots placed on high shelves. The old trick of filtering out a less than perfect view by growing trailing plants in pots on a shelf fixed across the top of the window so that the greenery trails down the glass is well tried and tested. Trailers can grow down from pots placed on small shelves or ornamental wall brackets, and they are perfect for high windows, which allow them to tumble down the wall below the sill. Smaller trailing plants can be grown around other plants in a grouped arrangement, where they can fill in the gaps between the plants and spill over the edges of the container, or they can be planted to cover the base and pot edges of large specimen plants. Plants with arching stems are ideal for display in a pot on a tall pedestal.

All of the following flourish in normal room temperatures unless otherwise indicated.

# plant directory

### Asparagus

Although they are often called ferns, the plants in the genus are evergreen and deciduous perennials, climbers and shrubs. *A. densiflorus* (asparagus fern) has arching stems with glossy, light green leaves. The cultivar 'Sprengeri' (syn. *A. sprengeri*; emerald feather) had arching stems. It is the larger, more common and more luxuriant of the two popular asparagus ferns, the other being 'Meyersii' (syn. *A. meyeri*; foxtail fern). The hanging stems of emerald feathers are covered with a froth of green needles and quickly grow to 1–1.2m (3–4ft). Grow in semi-shade with a minimum winter temperature of 8°C (48°F). These plants need high humidity, especially when the air is warm. Feed every two to three weeks from spring to autumn.

### Callisia elegans (striped inch plant)

Formerly known as *Setcreasea striata*, this is spreading perennial, with oval, dark green leaves with white, longitudinal stripes and purple beneath. White flowers are borne from autumn to winter. These are easy plants, tolerant of a wide range of conditions. Grow in bright or filtered light with a minimum winter temperature of 10°C (50°F). Water regularly during the growing season and feed once a month.

### Chlorophytum comosum (spider plant)

This well-known and easy-to-grow plant has arching green leaves and is best known in its striped forms 'Variegatum' and 'Vittatum'. Grow it where its white runners, up to 75cm (30in) long, with their little plantlets, can hang freely. It needs bright, indirect light and a minimum winter temperature of 7°C (45°F). Feed every week from spring to autumn and repot as soon as the roots fill the pot.

### Epipremnum aureum (devil's ivy, golden pothos)

Formerly (and still sometimes) known as *Scindapsus aureus*, this is a fast-growing plant with glossy, bright green, heart-shaped leaves that are splashed and spotted with creamy-white. It is a good plant for training up canes, a trellis or a mossy pole in either bright or dim light. Grow it in good but filtered light. It needs a minimum winter temperature of 15°C (60°F). Water plants freely during the spring and summer and feed once a month. In winter keep the compost just moist.

### Ficus pumila (creeping fig)

Formerly known as *F. reptans*, this relative of the rubber plant (see page 50) has small, glossy, heart-shaped leaves when young. Its shoots grow to 30cm (12in) per year. The cultivar 'Sonny' has white-edged leaves. Grow in semi-shade with a minimum winter temperature of 10°C (50°F). Water regularly during the growing season and feed once a month. These plants need high humidity.

*Opposite:* Two young plants of *Fittonia albivensis* Argyroneura Group are a fine contrast with *Spathiphdyllum wallisii* (peace lily).

*Above:* Like many plants with small, delicate leaves, *Ficus pumilla* 'Variegata' (creeping fig) looks at its best against a plain background.

### Fittonia albivensis (net leaf, nerve plant)

These evergreen, mat-forming perennials have small oval leaves, strongly veined in a contrasting colour. The leaves of *F. albivensis* Argyroneura Group (silver net leaf) are pale green with silver-white veining; those of Verschaffeltii Group (painted net leaf) are dark green with red veins. These are good plants for a terrarium. They need soil-less compost in indirect light. Maintain high humidity around the plants and provide a minimum temperature of 15°C (60°F). Do not allow the compost to get too wet, but feed every three to four weeks in the growing season.

### Glechoma hederacea 'Variegata' (creeping variegated ground ivy)

This plant used to be known as *Nepeta glechoma* 'Variegata (syn. *N. hederacea* 'Variegata'). It has white-splashed, scalloped leaves and grows best in cooler rooms. It grows well as a trailer and its stems can reach to 1.8m (6ft) if not kept trimmed. Grow in bright, indirect light with a winter temperature of no higher than 13°C (55°F). Keep the compost moist and feed once a week in summer.

### Gynura aurantica (velvet plant)

Sometimes (but wrongly) known and sold as *G. sarmentosa*, this woody perennial is upright at first, but increasingly becomes a trailer as it grows. The purple leaves are hairy, and the yellow-orange flowers appear during winter. It grows fast if it is given plenty of light, and the growing tip should be pinched out regularly in order to keep the plants bushy. Grow in bright, but filtered light, with a minimum winter temperature of 13°C (55°F). Water regularly during the growing season and feed every three to four weeks.

### Maranta leuconeura (prayer plant)

These attractive foliage plants have dark green, oval leaves, beautifully marked with shades of green, grey-green and silver. The undersides are reddish-purple. The cultivar 'Erythroneura' (herringbone plant) has wonderful leaves: they are dark green with a lighter central line, red veins and midribs and irregular, lighter green margins. 'Kerchoveana' has light green leaves with bold, dark green-brown splodges. 'Massangeana' has black-green leaves with silver-grey variegation, veins and midribs and purple undersides. Their common name derives from their habit of raising their leaves at night. All grow to about 30cm (12in) high and across. Grow in filtered light or semi-shade away from all draughts. They need high humidity and should be watered regularly in summer, with a liquid feed every three to four weeks. Reduce the water in winter. They need a minimum winter temperature of about 15°C (60°F). They have a trailing habit and can be grown in a hanging basket or trained up a moss pole.

### Philodendron scandens (sweetheart plant, heart leaf)

This popular and easy plant has glossy, heart-shaped leaves. It can be trained as a climber if you wish but also spreads and trails beautifully, with shoots growing as much as 0.6–1m (2–3ft) in a year. Grow in good, indirect light, although it will tolerate periods in shade. The temperature should never be higher than 24°C (75°F). Water generously from spring to autumn and feed once a week in summer.

### Plectranthus

The genus contains two trailing plants that make attractive houseplants, especially suitable for hanging baskets. *P. forsteri* (syn. *P. coleoides*) has light green leaves with scalloped edges; the cultivar 'Marginata' has leaves that are prettily edged with white. *P. oertendahlii* (candle plant) has bronze-green leaves with creamy-white veins and midribs; the undersides are purplish. Grow plants in good light but sheltered from strong, direct sun, and with a minimum winter temperature of 10°C (50°F). Water plants regularly during

*Above left:* Maranta *leuconeura* 'Erythroneura' (herringbone plant), like all the prayer plants, has leaves that point upwards at night.
*Above:* The trouble-free *Tradescantia pallida* 'Purpurea' (purple heart) can quickly become straggly, but it is easy to grow replacement plants from cuttings.
*Above right:* Its trailing habit and heart-shaped leaves make *Philodendron scandens* (sweetheart plant) perfect for hanging baskets. Here it is balanced visually by a *Nephrolepis cordifolia* (sword fern), a small-leaved trailing *Hedera helix* (ivy) and the white- and green-leaved *Plectranthus forsteri* 'Marginatus' (candle plant).

the growing season, feeding once a month, but give them less water during winter.

### Saxifraga stolonifera (mother of thousands)
This rosette-forming plant, previously known as *S. sarmentosa*, produces a mound of round, hairy leaves and produces wiry, pinkish runners up to 1m (3ft) long threaded with numerous little plantlets that can be potted up. The cultivar 'Tricolor' (syn. *S. stolonifera* 'Magic Carpet') has variegated leaves marked with white and flushed with pink in patches. Grow plants in good, indirect light with a minimum winter temperature of 10°C (50°F). Water from below, fairly generously in summer and more sparingly in winter. Feed every two to three weeks during summer.

### Scindapsus pictus 'Argyraeum'
Formerly (and confusingly) known as *Epipremnum pictum* 'Argyraeum', this is a slow-growing climber, with heart-shaped, velvety leaves covered in silvery spots. Grow plants in good but filtered light. They need a minimum winter temperature of 15°C (60°F).

Water freely during spring and summer and feed once a month. In winter keep the compost just moist.

### Tradescantia
*T. fluminensis* (wandering Jew), a trailing perennial, has oval, light green leaves, often purplish beneath. The cultivar 'Variegata' (syn. *T. albiflora* 'Variegata') has leaves that are longitudinally striped with white and green. *T. pallida* (syn. *Setcreasea pallida*; purple heart) is a tolerant plant, with long, narrow, purple leaves with a velvety bloom. The upright stems of young plants soon grow long and can become straggly, but it is easy to grow replacement plants from cuttings. *T. zebrina* (syn. *Zebrina pendula*; wandering Jew) is another trailing plant. It has blue-green leaves, longitudinally striped with purplish-pink and purplish-pink below. Grow in full sun. Plants need a normal summer room temperature, but a minimum winter temperature of 7–10°C (45–50°F). Water moderately in summer, sparingly in winter.

*Left: Syngonium podophyllum* (arrowhead vine) has attractively patterned leaves. Plants can be trained up moss poles or allowed to trail.
*Right:* Trained up canes, *Cissus antarctica* (kangaroo vine) soon develops into a substantial specimen for a large pot.
*Far right: Cissus rhombifolia* 'Ellen Danica' (mermaid vine) can be trained in a number of ways.

# climbing plants

In the wild climbing plants climb up, sprawl over or twine around a host by means of aerial roots, sprawling stems or curling tendrils. In the home, therefore, they need to be given some means of support. Plants with tendrils will soon cling to the support by their tendrils, but other types need to be tied in. Such climbers can equally well be left to their own devices,

given no support and not tied in, and grown as trailing plants – it is just a question of training. Most climbers will happily grow up a suitable cane, but plants with aerial roots can be grown up moss poles, and other climbers are often trained into ornamental shapes or up a trellis.

Climbing foliage plants include some of the most tolerant plants, and can be used

in many decorative ways. Stately, larger leaved plants, such as *Philodendron domesticum* (elephant's ear), which produces large, fleshy, aerial roots, make a strong statement and are often best in isolation, growing slowly to great height over the years. Scramblers, such as *Cissus rhombifolia* (grape ivy), will travel a long way in a short time and can be trained in many styles.

## plant directory

**Cissus**
*C. antarctica* (kangaroo vine) has a mass of tooth-edged, glossy green leaves and is tolerant of poor light. As a young plant it is normally grown up a group of canes, but when it is older it can be trained over a trellis. It is vigorous and can be trimmed back at any time of year to keep it within reasonable bounds.
*C. discolor* (begonia vine) has pointed leaves, which are dark green

zoned with silver, grey and pink above and dark red underneath. It can become straggly.
*C. rhombifolia* (syn. *Rhoicissus rhombifolia*; grape ivy) is a long-lived plant with a mass of glossy, dark green leaves, which are strongly veined and toothed. It bears greenish flowers, which are followed by blue-black berries. It will tolerate some shade but really does best in a fairly bright light. It needs plenty of room

and grows well over a trellis or around a doorway.
Grow these plants in bright or filtered light with a minimum winter temperature of 5°C (10°F). Water regularly during the growing season and feed once a month. Water less often in winter.

**x *Fatshedera lizei*** (tree ivy)
Although this can be grown in the garden in mild areas, it makes a

handsome houseplant that is easy to look after, eventually growing to about 3m (10ft). The large, glossy, dark green leaves are shaped like ivy leaves. A variegated form, 'Variegata', has leaves edged with cream, but this is less vigorous and less hardy than the species. Plants need a support to grow around. Grow in good light, protecting variegated plants from strong, direct sun. Water regularly during the growing season, feeding monthly, but reduce water in winter.

### Hedera (ivy)

*H. canariensis* (Canary island ivy) is an undemanding plant, usually grown in its variegated form 'Gloire de Marengo'. This has green and white leaves, is easily trained as a climber and is a good choice for draughty halls. It must have reasonably cool conditions, with adequate light. Small-growing cultivars of *H. helix* that are suitable for unheated rooms include 'White Knight' (syn. 'Helvig'), which has small, white-variegated leaves, and 'Melanie', which has leaves that have light purple, slightly crimped margins. Grow in good but indirect light. Water ivies regularly during the growing season, feeding once a month, and keep the compost just moist in winter.

### Philodendron domesticum (elephant's ear)

This climber, formerly known as *P. hastatum*, can grow to 6m (20ft) in a greenhouse but is a more modest 1.5m (5ft) in a pot. It needs a big moss pole and a position in semi-shade. Water freely during the growing season and feed every three to four weeks. In winter maintain a minimum temperature of 15°C (60°F) and keep the compost just moist.

### Syngonium podophyllum (goosefoot, arrowhead vine)

Formerly known as *Nephthytis triphylla*, goosefoot is a fleshy-leaved climber with aerial roots ideal for training up a moss pole. Many cultivars have variegated leaves, including 'White Butterfly'. 'Emerald Gem' has large, fleshy, spade-shaped leaves. Grow in good light, providing variegated plants with shade from strong sunlight. Maintain high humidity and water freely in the growing season, feeding every three to four weeks, but keep the compost just moist in winter. These plants need a minimum winter temperature of 15°F (60°F).

# upright plants

Large architectural plants really come into their own when they stand alone and are displayed as specimen plants in large pots on the floor. The container you use makes all the difference. For large plants it is usually best to have a container that is a quarter to a third the height of the plant and that is in a shape and style that both flatters the plant and complements the furniture and decor of the room. As the plant grows you will need to repot it into a pot one size larger from time to time to prevent it from becoming pot bound. This makes an opportunity to change the cache pot or container to keep it in proportion with the plant.

Plants that are too big to be repotted should be top-dressed – the top 2.5–5cm (1–2in) of the compost is removed annually and replaced with fresh compost, which provides a supply of nutrients and aerates the compost.

Smaller plants with bold forms and patterned leaves, such as the easy *Solenostemon* (coleus) and more demanding *Codiaeum variegatum* var. *pictum* (croton), also look good standing on the floor where you can look down on their leaves, and these plants benefit from being planted in groups of two or three forms together to show off their contrasting leaf coloration. You can also make a floor group of assorted foliage plants of differing heights with a mixture of leaf shapes, colours and forms.

There is often least light at floor level. Fortunately, there are plenty of suitable foliage plants – the many calatheas and marantas, for example – that need shade. Plants that need more light can be raised by, for instance, using a planting trough on legs. Standing plants on the floor is ideal for attic rooms with low windows or for rooms with overhead lighting, where bright light reaches down to floor level. However, having too many pots standing on the floor can be unwelcome when you have to clean around them or move them in order to clean, and having a single container is often the best solution in all but a conservatory room. Alternatively, a low platform on casters, which can be moved for cleaning, will enable you to make a floor-level grouping of plants.

*Left:* Contrasting types of foliage can be exploited to the full in a mixed bowl. The smooth, shapely leaves of *Aspidistra elatior* 'Variegata' (cast iron plant) are offset by a haze of *Asparagus densiflorus* Sprengeri Group (asparagus fern).
*Right:* *Begonia rex* hybrids are grown for their foliage rather than their usually insignificant flowers. They tend to look best in plain pots.

# plant directory

**Aspidistra elatior** **(cast iron plant)**
This well-known indoor plant has long been a favourite for growing in the home. The glossy, dark green leaves are lance-shaped and can grow to 50cm (20in) long. These are tolerant plants, at home in a bright light or semi-shade. Water freely during the growing season, feeding once a month, and reduce the amount of water in winter. They need a minimum winter temperature of about 7°C (45°F).

### Begonia
This important genus includes some fine foliage plants. *B. rex* (king begonia, painted-leaf begonia) is a perennial with handsome metallic green leaves that have a broad, silvery band around the margins and pink and purple tones around the darker centre. The undersides of the leaves are brownish-red. Many cultivars, known as Rex-cultorum begonias, have been developed, all with brilliantly coloured foliage. These plants generally grow to about 25in (10in) high and 30cm (12in) across.
    *B. masoniana* (iron-cross begonia)

is another fine foliage plant, although it does bear clusters of insignificant greenish-white flowers in summer. The leaves, which are to 20cm (8in) long, have a puckered surface. They are green or yellowish-green and are strongly marked with a black-brown central pattern, resembling the German Iron Cross. Plants get to about 45cm (18in) high and across.
    These begonias need good but filtered light and a minimum winter temperature of 10°C (50°F). Never overwater and maintain a humid atmosphere by standing pots in trays filled with clay granules, gravel or the like. Feed every two to three weeks during the growing season and keep the compost just moist in winter. Pot on in spring into good quality potting compost.

### Calathea
There are several handsome foliage plants in the genus, the best known and most widely available being *C. makoyana* (syn. *Maranta makoyana*; cathedral windows, peacock plant). The leaves, which grow to 30cm (12in) long, have dark

green central areas surrounded by lighter green with mid-green margins and veining. The undersides are purplish. Plants grow to 45cm (18in) high and about 23cm (9in) across.
    *C. sanderiana* (syn. *C. majestica* 'Sanderiana', *C. ornata* var. *sanderiana*) has dark green leaves, potentially to 60cm (2ft) long, strongly striped with red-pink, fading to creamy-white. The undersides are purplish. Plants can grow to 3m (10ft) in the wild, although container-grown plants rarely reach that size.
    *C. zebrina* (zebra plant) has dark green, oval leaves, to 45cm (18in) long, which are edged and veined with mid-green. Plants grow to 1m (3ft) high and 60cm (2ft) across.
    Calatheas are not easy to grow. They tolerate fairly low levels of light but must never stand in a draught. They need an even temperature, with a winter minimum of 16°C (61°F), and a constantly humid atmosphere. Mist and water freely during the growing season and feed once a month. In winter the compost should be kept just moist.

## Codiaeum variegatum var. pictum (croton)

A large number of colourful cultivars
has been developed from this foliage
plant. The narrowly oval, glossy,
rather leathery leaves, to 30cm (12in)
long, are usually mid-green splashed
with yellow, ageing to shades of red.
The young, mid-green leaves of
'Flamingo' have cream-coloured
veins, turning yellow and ageing to
red or purple. The striking leaves of
'Evening Embers' are blue-black, with
red veining and red and green marks.
Plants can grow to about 1m (3ft)
high and to 60cm (2ft) or more across.

All crotons must be kept out of
draughts. They need a minimum
winter temperature of 10°C (50°F)
and a position in good light but out
of any strong, direct sunlight. Water
freely during the growing season,
misting frequently and feeding every
two to three weeks. In winter keep
the compost just moist, using tepid
water. Crotons are particularly
susceptible to scale insect and red
spider mite.

## Cordyline (cabbage palm)

Many cordylines come from Australia
and New Zealand, and although some
of the larger forms can occasionally
be grown outside in mild areas, they
are best regarded as foliage
houseplants. All cordylines have an
erect central stem from which sword-
shaped or lance-shaped leaves are
borne. *C. fruticosa* (syn. *C. terminalis*;
good luck tree, ti tree) has dark green
leaves, which can grow to 60cm (2ft)
long. These plants can achieve
heights of 5m (15ft), although this is
unlikely in a container. There are
many colourful cultivars, including
'Baby Ti', which has leaves that are
boldly edged in red; this is a good
choice for indoors because it grows
to only 60cm (2ft) high and across.
'Tricolor' has leaves that are boldly
splashed with green, reddish-pink
and cream.

*C. stricta* is lower growing and
has more arching leaves. The species
has dark green leaves, but those of
the cultivar 'Rubra' are flushed with
red and those of 'Discolor' are
bronze-purple.

Cordylines need a bright position,
although variegated forms do best in
filtered light. Water regularly in the
growing season, feeding once a
month, and reduce the amount of
water in winter. They need a
minimum winter temperature of
about 10°C (50°F).

## Dieffenbachia seguine (dumb cane)

The species is also sometimes
available as *D. amoena* and
*D. maculata*. All dieffenbachias exude
a sap that can irritate the skin; do not
touch your mouth or eyes if you have
been handling one of these plants.
There are several cultivars, all with
handsome, oval leaves, which are
variably patterned in white, cream
and shades of green. The cultivar
'Amoena' has creamy-white bands
and marbling; 'Exotica' has dark green
leaves with bold white and greenish-
white marks; 'Maculata' has bright
green leaves with creamy-white veins
and splodges. All these plants grow to
about 60cm (2ft) high and across.

Dieffenbachias need a bright
position but sheltered from strong,
direct sun and high humidity. Water
and mist freely in summer, feeding
every three to four weeks, and reduce
the water in winter. Plants need a
minimum winter temperature of
15°C (60°F).

## Dracaena

Plants in the genus are similar to
cordylines; indeed, much renaming
has occurred between the two
genera, and plants offered for sale as

belonging to one genus may well belong to the other. Dracaenas are architectural plants, which look splendid grown on their own where their overall shape can be admired. *D. fragrans* is an erect plant, growing to 15m (50ft) tall in the wild and with leaves to 1.2m (4ft) long. There are several cultivars more suitable for growing indoors. Plants in Deremensis Group have leaves that are variegated in various ways: 'Lemon Lime', for instance, has lime green leaves with yellow edges and central lines; 'Warneckei' has dark grey-green leaves with white stripes.

*D. marginata* (Madagascar dragon tree) has red-edged, dark green leaves; it will grow to 5m (15ft) tall. The cultivar 'Tricolor' has narrow leaves that are edged with red and creamy-white.

*D. sanderiana* (ribbon plant) is a slender plant, growing ultimately to 1.5m (5ft) tall. The narrow leaves are glossy green with silver-white stripes. An added attraction is that the leaves are slightly wavy.

Dracaenas need to be grown in good light, although plants will all-green leaves will tolerate some shade. They need a minimum winter temperature of about 13°C (55°F). Water freely throughout the growing season, feeding every three to four weeks. Reduce the amount of water in winter.

**Fatsia japonica (Japanese aralia)**
Also known as *Aralia japonica*, this is a large, handsome plant, which can be grown in gardens in mild areas, where it will grow to 4m (12ft) high and across; plants rarely achieve those dimensions in containers. The large, dark green, glossy leaves are deeply divided into 7–11 lobes and can be to 40cm (16in) long. In autumn little creamy-white flowers appear, and these are followed by round black fruit. There is an attractive variegated form, 'Variegata', which has leaves with broad cream margins; it is less hardy than the species. Grown as houseplants, fatsias need good light, although variegated plants should be protected from strong summer sun. Water regularly during the growing season, feeding every three to four weeks, but reduce the water in winter.

### Ficus (fig)

The genus contains two handsome but quite different looking, upright foliage plants, in addition to the smaller *F. pumila* (see page 41). *F. benjamina* (weeping fig) is a small tree with fluttering, dark green leaves on weeping branches. Although weeping figs grow to 30m (100ft) in the wild, container-grown plants are usually about 1.8m (6ft) tall. There are a number of cultivars: 'Exotica' has leaves with extended, twisted tips; the leaves of 'Starlight' have gold-coloured variegations; 'Variegata' has white-edged leaves.

While the leaves of *F. benjamina* are 5–13cm (2–5in) long, those of *F. elastica* (rubber plant, India rubber tree) can be 45cm (18in) long. They are dark, glossy green, often flushed with red and prominently ribbed, and they have a leathery texture. In the wild *F. elastica* can achieve heights of up to 60m (200ft), but as a houseplant a height of 3m (10ft) is more usual. Cultivars are available from time to

time: the leaves of 'Decora' have cream ribs and are reddish beneath; the grey-green leaves of 'Doescheri' are variegated with creamy-white and yellow; 'Robusta' has large leaves opening from red or orange shoots.

Grow in good light but shaded from strong, direct sun. These plants need a minimum winter temperature of 15°C (55°F). Water regularly during the growing season, taking care that the compost does not become waterlogged, and give a high-nitrogen feed once a month. Keep the compost just moist in winter.

### Monstera deliciosa (Swiss cheese plant)

This well-known houseplant has large, glossy, dark green leaves. When they are young, the leaves are heart-shaped, but as they age they develop large oblong holes between the veins. In its native Central America it is a huge plant, but in a container a plant will grow to about 3m (10ft) tall. Plants grow well when they are supported

*Below left: Schefflera arboricola* grows quickly to a height of 1.5–1.8m (5–6ft). to form a bushy plant. Its leaves consist of leaflets radiating on parasol 'spokes' from the tips of leaf-stalks.
*Below: Ficus elastica* (rubber plant) are good, bold specimens to stand in pots on the floor.
*Right: Monstera deliciosa* (Swiss cheese plant) has large, leathery leaves, which develop holes like Swiss cheese as they grow.
*Far right: Yucca elephantipes* makes a permanent houseplant feature. Bold plants such as this need sturdy pots, both visually and to take their weight. This yucca produces leaves to 1m (3ft) long.

on a moss pole, and mature plants develop aerial roots, which can be trained into the moss or down into the compost. They are tolerant of a range of conditions but do best in a bright position, shaded from strong, direct sunlight, and with high humidity. Water well throughout the growing period, feeding every three to four weeks, but reduce the amount of water in winter.

### Schefflera

*S. actinophylla* (syn. *Brassaia actinophylla*; octopus tree, Australian ivy palm) has large, bright green leaves divided into leaflets that are borne in rosettes at the end of the leaf stalks, so that they resemble a parasol. The young plants that are available as houseplants can reach 3m (10ft), although in the wild they will get to 12m (40ft) or more.

   *S. arboricola* (syn. *Heptapleurum arboricola*) grows to 1m (3ft). It has glossy green leaves, divided into 7–16 arching leaflets, which surround the leaf stalk. The form 'Variegata' has yellow-variegated leaves.

   *S. elegantissima* (syn. *Aralia elegantissima, Dizygotheca elegantissima*; false aralia) is an attractive but difficult plant. The dark green-brown, glossy leaves are finely divided and are flushed with bronze beneath; the midribs are white. In the right position plants will grow to 3m (10ft) tall.

   Scheffleras should be grown in good light but sheltered from direct sun. The need a minimum winter temperature of about 13°C (55°F). Water regularly throughout the growing season, feeding every three to four weeks, but keep just moist in winter. These plants do not like being moved around, so once you have found a spot that suits your plant, try to keep it there.

### Solenostemon scutellarioides (coleus, flame nettle)

Formerly sold as *Coleus blumei* var. *verschaffeltii*, these bushy plants have brightly coloured foliage, often vividly patterned, in shades of green, yellow, orange, red and brown. Pinch out the growing tips to keep plants bushy. They will grow to about 60cm (2ft) high and across. They need a fairly light position, but away from direct sun, and a minimum winter temperature of 4°C (39°F). Water freely in the growing season and feed every two weeks. Keep compost just moist in winter and pot on in spring.

### Yucca

The genus contains plants that can be grown outside in mild areas, but *Y. elephantipes* (syn. *Y. gigantea, Y. guatemalensis*; boundary plant, spineless yucca) is a popular indoor plant, growing to 1.8m (6ft) high. It needs good light and fairly cool winter conditions, with a winter minimum of 10°C (50°F). Water freely during the growing season, feeding once a month, and keep the compost just moist in winter. If well cared for it will eventually produce white flowers.

*Left: Capsicum annuum* (ornamental pepper) are cheerful plants for autumn and winter with their brightly coloured fruits. They do best in direct light where several of the plants arranged together will make a colourful show.

*Right: Nertera depressa* (bead plant) is usually grown as a pot plant for its bright autumn and winter berries. It needs bright light, cool air and plenty of summer moisture. If given a dry, late winter rest, and a spring and summer outdoors, it will produce its shiny 'beads' year after year.

*Far right: Fortunella japonica* (kumquat) is highly decorative if rather temperamental. Given plenty of light, warmth and moisture, it will produce attractive fruit.

# berried & fruiting plants

Some of the most decorative houseplants are grown for their fruits or berries. Fruiting plants can give double value, some having beautiful, fragrant flowers, as well but in general, plants with attractive berries, such as

*Nertera depressa* (bead plant), have negligible flowers.

Most fruiting plants require extra care, especially those with edible fruit, such as miniature orange, lemon and kumquat. They need a conservatory or at

least an airy, sunny room, and do not produce fruit without the right amount of warmth, light and humidity. However, some of the best ornamental fruiting plants, such as *Capsicum annuum*, are easily grown as annuals.

# plant directory

**Capsicum annuum (ornamental peppers)**
These plants are grown as annuals. They come in many colours, from red and yellow to white, purple and black, all starting off green. Sow the seed in spring, cover the seed tray and keep at a temperature of 21°C (70°F). Germination takes about two weeks. Pot up as the plants grow and pinch out at the tips to make them bushy and fruitful. Give plenty of humidity, water well and feed once a fortnight as peppers appear.

**Citrus limon (lemon)**
Many members of the genus can be grown as houseplants, and it is possible to obtain fruit from many, but this species is one of the most widely available. It grows into a large, spiny shrub with light green leaves and, in summer, fragrant white flowers. The yellow fruit follow the flowers. The cultivar 'Meyeri' (syn. *C. meyeri*; Meyer's lemon) is similar but bears small, ornamental lemon fruits. Grow in good light but shade from direct summer sun. Mist and water freely, feeding every two to

three weeks in the growing season. Reduce the water in winter and maintain a temperature above 5°C (41°F). Plants benefit from standing outside during the summer.

**x Citrofortunella microcarpa (calamondin, Panama orange)**
Formerly known as *C. mitis*, this large shrub grows slowly to a height of 1m (3ft). If it is well watered in summer, given plenty of light all year and a cool, 13°C (55°F), winter rest, it should produce white, scented, waxy flowers and small, edible fruit. Even if it fails to flower it is an attractive, bushy, evergreen shrub.

**Ficus deltoidea (mistletoe fig)**
The small, slow-growing shrub has grey-gold, sometimes red-flushed, berries borne singly on little stems sprouting from the leaf-joints. The dark green leaves are small and oval. Plants usually grow to 45–75cm (18–30in) across and 45cm (18in) across, although it can grow much bigger if kept in a tub. The plant will stand a winter low temperature of 10°C (50°F).

**Fortunella japonica (kumquat)**
This large, spiny shrub has glossy green leaves and fragrant flowers in spring and summer. These are followed by the small golden-yellow fruits. Grow in good light with a winter minimum temperature of 7°C (45°F).

**Nertera depressa (bead plant)**
This is a stem-rooting, spreading perennial, to 2.5cm (1in) high, with bright green leaves. In summer it produces yellow-green flowers, and these are followed by a mass of small orange or red berries. Grow in filtered light and water freely during the growing season, feeding once a month. Water less often in winter.

**Solanum capsicastrum (winter cherry)**
This plant has nothing to do with cherries and the shining, berries, which turn from green through yellow to orange or red in winter, are poisonous. Do not overwater and keep in a cool room at 10–15°C (50–60°F) but in bright light. *S. pseudocapsicum* (Christmas cherry) is similar but has larger berries.

# 5 PALMS, FERNS & BROMELIADS

Palms, ferns and bromeliads are not, of course, related plants, but they all have, in their own ways, highly distinctive foliage and something exotic about them. All three groups of plants make fine and worthwhile houseplants.

Most of the palms grown as houseplants are tropical or subtropical plants that require warmth and humidity and bright but filtered light, although there are some, such as *Chamaedorea elegans* (parlour palm) and the much larger *Howea forsteriana* (kentia palm), that will tolerate ordinary, fluctuating living-room conditions. A palm takes dedication and time to produce, and it is a long-term investment, to be chosen with care and looked after equally carefully.

Ferns have been popular since Victorian times, when they were collected and housed in glass cases or in glass ferneries built on outdoor balconies. They can look exotically redolent of the jungle or be light and fragile. Ferns from temperate regions are often less than ideal as houseplants, because they require cooler conditions than centrally heated homes can offer, but numerous tropical and subtropical ferns flourish in the temperatures we prefer for ourselves as long as they are given plenty of humidity and are not subjected to sudden temperature changes.

In the wild many bromeliads grow on other plants or on rocks, taking their nourishment from the air and from organic debris, although a few root in shallow soil. Many species will adapt to being grown in pots indoors as exotic plants, and although they are grown as foliage plants some occasionally produce spectacular flowers. Others can be grown on stones and driftwood or up moss poles, and some are suitable for hanging baskets.

While palms and ferns and some types of bromeliad are coming back into fashion after a period of neglect, some bromeliads have only recently been introduced to cultivation as houseplants. Many of these plants have to be sought out, as only the most popular are widely available. Some palms, especially young ones, can be bought from nurseries and garden centres and even the plant sections of large supermarkets and chain stores, but others will have to be obtained from specialist houseplant growers. Commoner ferns and bromeliads can also be found in many garden centres and other shops, but the more unusual specimens of these plants have to be obtained from specialist growers.

*Opposite*: A large conservatory is a stunning setting for a few large specimen plants.
*Above: Phoenix canariensis* (Canary Island date palm) makes a striking architectural plant.

# palms

Palms are widely associated with ideas of elegance and splendour and of exotic lands. They make us think of oases in the hot, dry desert and palm-fringed beaches of white sand or even of the palm courts and palm court orchestras of fashionable watering places of days gone by.

In Victorian and Edwardian times the most demanding and largest palms were grown in glass houses, where they could be given the warmth and lush humidity they needed. Surprisingly, perhaps, the resilient fronds of the most tolerant species swayed over the

comings and goings in hotel foyers and restaurants in all sorts of public rooms. The entrance halls and drawing rooms of late nineteenth- and early twentieth-century homes were also often graced with parlour palms.

As simpler styles replaced the opulence and clutter and dim

light of Victorian and Edwardian interiors, palms went out of fashion, but now they have found their way back into our homes in interiors of a different style. With its well-defined fronds and stark but graceful shape, a palm is an outstanding plant, which makes a striking feature and one that is especially well suited to a large, bright, plainly furnished and decorated interior.

Traditionally, palms were displayed on ceramic palm stands, with the palm planted in an ornamental jardinière balanced on top of a matching pedestal. Displaying them in this way, using original or reproduction palm stands (both of which are expensive), is perfect for a room in a period house decorated in the appropriate style. But it could also successfully supply an unusual feature in an otherwise simple, modern interior. Any pedestal or pedestal table is a good way of giving prominence to the smaller palms, but a large palm generally looks best standing on the floor in a pot or cache pot of good quality, and it will, in any case, be too heavy to be raised on any kind of stand. Containers can be patterned porcelain, glazed earthenware, brass or copper, basketware or even plain, well-made plastic planters, depending on the setting.

Palms grow in two rather extreme situations: in arid deserts and in lush, green jungles. Either of these can be expressed in the way the plants are displayed. Palms in a bare room, with polished or varnished wooden floors, echo the idea of plants growing in a barren, desert landscape, but palms

growing with other foliage plants, perhaps in a room with a green carpet or a green-patterned wallpaper, bring out the tropical jungle theme. This can also be achieved in miniature with a group of foliage plants, such as foliage begonias, selaginellas and small ferns, grown in a glass case with a small, young palm, such as *Chamaedorea elegans* or *Lytocaryum weddellianum* (Weddell palm).

Perhaps more than any other plant, palms lend themselves to creating shadows and reflections. A palm standing in an alcove that is lined with a mirror creates a stunning effect, and one each side of a fireplace reflected in this way is doubly stunning. The shadows cast by a palm's fronds can pattern a plain wall in a most dramatic way. Spotlights create a good strong light for bold shadows but generate heat so should not be positioned too close to the plant. Lighting the plant from below creates shadows on the ceiling as well as the walls, and a plain blind (as opposed to a curtain) provides a good, smooth surface for shadows.

*Above left*: Palms are are long-lived. *Howea forsteriana* (kentia palm), creates a dramatic feature (left), and *Chamaedorea elegans* (parlour palm), has a feathery outline (right). *Above*: *Phoenix canariensis* (Canary Island date palm) will make an eye-catching focal point. Its graceful foliage looks best against a plain background.

*Left*: Although *Howea forsteriana* (kentia palm) will eventually become a large plant, it retains the lightness and grace shown by this small young specimen. A window position is ideal for winter, but some shade from summer sun is needed.

*Right: Dypsis lutescens* (areca palm) may be sold as butterfly palm, yellow palm, golden feather palm, yellow butterfly palm, cane palm and golden cane palm. It enjoys temperatures of 13–16°C (55–61°F) in winter and up to 27°C (80°F) in summer.

## CARE AND CULTIVATION

In the wild many – although not all – palms grow to great heights, but in the main they are slow-growing plants and can remain at living-room size for many years. These are not plants for impatient indoor gardeners. New fronds unfurl in a leisurely way at the rate of only two or three a year. In many of the palms grown as houseplants several fronds are produced from ground, or compost, level, whereas the large palms, which generally require extremely high temperatures – *Phoenix* (date palms), for example – have a single stem (the trunk) with a flourish of fronds at the top. A frond is really a compound leaf and each apparent leaf is really a leaflet, forming part of the whole frond. In each frond, all the growth develops from a single growth point, known as the terminal bud, and if this is damaged the whole frond is affected. If you cut a stem it will not re-grow. Palms are among the few plants that grow best in relatively small containers.

The most popular palms are adaptable specimens. They like a winter rest in cooler conditions, although not normally in temperatures below about 10°C (50°F), but they tolerate central heating. They prefer good but not strong light, especially when young (in the wild they would be growing in the shade of other, taller plants), but can survive in quite dim corners. They dislike draughts and sudden changes of temperature, although some prefer a regular slight drop in temperature at night.

Palms grow best if their roots are allowed to fill the pot, and they should not be repotted unnecessarily. They need a soil-based potting compost, with plenty of drainage material at the bottom of the pot. In summer, or in warm rooms, they need plenty of watering, but in lower temperatures the compost should be allowed to dry out a little between waterings. The plants should never be allowed to become waterlogged and must not stand with their pots in any excess water that has drained out. They should be regularly fed in summer. Palms appreciate humid conditions, and they should be misted frequently in warm rooms. They can also be stood on a tray of wet pebbles to keep the atmosphere humid. The fronds should be cleaned from time to time by being wiped with a cloth that has been wrung out in tepid water.

Palms are sensitive to chemicals and will be damaged if exposed to aerosol sprays. If you need to treat them with insecticides make sure that these are suitable for palms.

*Left: Chamaedorea elegans*
(the parlour palm) has a
more feathery outline than
many of the kentia palms.
*Above: Cycas revoluta*
(Japanese sago palm) is not
a true palm, although it is
often sold as one in garden
centres. Its strong, fan-like
fronds sprout from a
conical base, which is part
of its attraction.
*Right: Rhapsis excelsa*
(miniature fan palm) has
erect stems and spreading,
fan-shaped leaves.

# plant directory

### Caryota (fishtail palm)
These palms come from India, Sri
Lanka, Southeast Asia and Australia,
and the unusual leaves are more like
those of a fern than a palm. In the
wild they can grow to 12m (40ft) tall,
but container-grown specimens
generally grow to a maximum of 3m
(10ft). *C. mitis* (Burmese fish-tail palm,
clustered fish-tail palm) has mid-green
leaves, with lopsided leaflets. *C. urens*

(jaggery palm, sago palm, toddy palm,
wine palm) has dark green, arching
leaves, which are irregularly toothed.

### Chamaedorea
These Central and South American
palms have bamboo-like stems and
pinnate leaves. *C. elegans* (syn.
*Neanthe bella*; parlour palm, dwarf
mount palm) has mid-green leaves, to
1.2m (4ft) long, formed of 21–40

narrow leaflets. Plants will grow to 3m
(10ft). The cultivar 'Bella' is more
compact, growing slowly to 1m (3ft).
*C. metallica* (miniature fish-tail palm)
grows to 1m (3ft) tall and about 50cm
(20in) across. The blue-green leaves
are shaped like a fish's tail. *C. seifrizii*
(reed palm) is a small, clump-forming
plant, growing to about 1.8m (6ft)
high, with mid-green leaves, to 60cm
(2ft) long, composed of 24–28 leaflets.

### Chamaerops humilis (dwarf fan palm)

This palm, which is native to the western Mediterranean, is suitable for a cool conservatory or even an unheated porch. It will grow to no more than about 1.5m (5ft) tall. The fan-shaped leaves, with 12–15 leaflets, are blue-green or grey-green.

### Cycas (fern palm, sago palm)

These plants – cycads rather than true palms – are from Madagascar, Southeast Asia and Australia, and they produce whorls or rosettes of stiff leaves and stout, woody trunks. They make fine architectural plants but need space to look their best. *C. circinalis* (false sago, fern palm, sago palm) is slow growing, eventually getting to 1.8m (6ft) in a container. The glossy, dark green leaves are composed of up to 100 leaflets. *C revoluta* (Japanese sago palm) will grow to about 1.5m (5ft) in a container. It develops a stout trunk, with the leaves, to 75cm (30in) long, crowded in a rosette at the top.

### Dypsis lutescens (areca palm)

Formerly known as *Chrysalidocarpus lutescens* (syn. *Areca lutescens*), this small palm is also known as the yellow palm, butterfly palm and the golden feather palm. It is native to Madagascar, where it grows to 6m (20ft) tall, but in a container it will grow to 3m (10ft) or so. The arching leaves can grow to as much as 1.8m (6ft) long, even on container-grown plants. They are formed of numerous linear leaflets, which are usually yellow-green.

### Howea (sentry palm)

The two species in the genus originated on Lord Howe Island. The popular *H. belmoreana* (syn. *Kentia belmoreana*; curly palm) will grow to about 3m (10ft). The leaves, to 1m (3ft) long, arch strongly. The widely available *H. forsteriana* (syn. *Kentia forsteriana*; kentia palm, thatch leaf palm) will also grow to about 3m (10ft) tall in a container. The leaves have long-stalked leaflets, which point downwards at the end.

### Lytocaryum weddellianum (Weddell palm)

Formerly known as *Microcoelum weddellianum* (syn. *Syagrus weddelliana*), this palm from Brazil has an erect stem and leaves, to 1.2m (4ft) long, with red-black scales.

### Phoenix

These palms come from tropical and subtropical Asia and Africa. *P. canariensis* (Canary Island date palm) has flat, finely divided, feather-like leaves arising from a dense crown. The date palm, *P. dactylifera*, is quicker-growing than *P. canariensis* and has grey-green leaves with small leaflets; it is easily raised from date stones. *P. roebelenii* (miniature date palm, pygmy date palm) has glossy, dark green, arching leaves.

### Rhapsis (lady palm)

*Rhapsis excelsa* (syn. *R. flabelliformis*, miniature fan palm) will grow to about 1.5m (5ft) in a container. It has dark green, lustrous, deeply lobed leaves, with three to ten leaflets. *R. humilis* is a smaller, slimmer palm, with leaves that are composed of between 9 and 20 leaflets.

### Trachycarpus fortunei (windmill palm, Chusan palm)

This single-stemmed palm has large, fan-shaped, dark green leaves, which are deeply divided into many pleated segments and the leaf stalks are covered in fine teeth. This palm will survive outdoors in a very sheltered garden, but it must be protected from cold, drying winds to survive the winter. Indoors it will tolerate both bright sun and semi-shade.

### Washingtonia

There are two palms in the genus, which are native to southwestern United States and northern Mexico. *W. filifera* (syn. *W. filamentosa*; desert fan palm, petticoat palm) grows to 15m (50ft) ormore in the wild but to 1.8m (6ft) in a container, where it rarely forms a trunk. It is quite short-lived. The leaves have white filaments on the margins and the stem has coarse teeth. *W. robusta* (syn. *W. gracilis*, *Pritchardia robusta*; Mexican washingtonia) has bright green leaves and grows to about 1.8m (6ft) or so in a container. It has a more upright habit than *W. filifera* and is more slender.

*Left:* Ferns and baskets go well together. The arching, wiry stems of *Adiantum capillus-veneris* (maidenhair fern) bend over the basket's edge and reach towards the handle. A begonia adds colour and highlights the fern's light foliage.
*Above:* Ferns flourish when grown in a group, and smaller ferns can be planted together. Different species and cultivars of *Pteris* offer a range of foliage shapes and shades of green.
*Right:* The sedately arching fronds of a mature *Nephrolepis exaltata* 'Whitmonii' are seen at their best on a plant stand.

# ferns

Ferns are not difficult to grow, but draughts, dry air and extremes of temperature will do them no good at all. A fern that is pampered and protected from these ills will reward its owner with a wealth of luxuriant green fronds all year round.

There are many species of tropical and subtropical ferns, but there are also many ferns that are native to areas with temperate climates. These are well-suited to cooler parts of the house but will not survive in rooms that are too well heated. Tropical ferns are at home in warmer air and are better suited to centrally heated homes.

All ferns thrive on moisture and must be given humid conditions. In living rooms this usually means standing them on trays of damp pebbles or clay granules or putting each fern's pot in a larger pot and packing the gap with peat that is kept moist. Ferns should also be misted regularly with tepid, soft water unless the humidity of the whole room is kept high through the use of a humidifier.

Providing the right compost is also important, because most ferns are forest or woodland plants and have tender, delicate roots adapted to the light forest soil, which is rich in leaf mould and decayed vegetable matter.

*Left:* The height of *Asplenium scolopendrium* (hart's-tongue fern) makes an excellent background for low-growing or trailing plants. The Cristatum Group ferns have particularly attractive fronds, which are branched and crested.

## CARE AND CULTIVATION

The first requirement for ferns is a light, moisture-retaining compost, but it must be freely draining so that the roots are never waterlogged. A compost based on peat, or fibrous peat substitute, containing plenty of fine sand and small, sharp stones, is best. The compost should never be allowed to dry out, and this may mean giving plants a little water every day in a warm, dry atmosphere.

Although ferns grow in moist, shady places, this does not mean that they need no light. Their normal situation in the wild is dappled light, and light levels that are too low cause poor growth and yellowing fronds. Give ferns a position near to a window that gets morning or late afternoon sun or somewhere that receives good light within the room. Do, however, keep them away from strong sunlight, particularly during the summer, as it will soon make them lose their intense colouring and turn them a pallid or greyish-green, and it can also scorch their fronds, making them brown and dry around the edges.

Ferns can be kept in dim light as long as they are given regular holidays in bright light. They can also be given artificial light, but this should be from a special bulb or a fluorescent strip, because ordinary light bulbs generate too much heat.

Temperature is just as important as light and growing medium, but this depends on the individual fern's place of origin and adaptability. As a rule, most ferns dislike cold; ferns from temperate regions thrive at 10–15°C (50–60°F) – slightly cooler than most heated rooms – and those from tropical and subtropical areas need an average of 15–21°C (60–70°F). Most ferns like a winter rest at slightly lower temperatures, but few will survive at temperatures lower than 7°C (45°F), and for many ferns 10°C (50°F) is the absolute minimum.

In summer feed ferns every two to four weeks with weak liquid fertilizer. Do not mix to full strength because this can damage the delicate root systems. A few drops of fertilizer can be added occasionally to the water used for misting. Ferns should not be fed in winter if they are given a resting period. Mist as often as you like to keep the air around ferns moist, but never in low temperatures, at night or when the plant is standing in bright sunlight.

Repot ferns in spring, but only when their roots are filling the pot. Otherwise, simply gently scrape out and replace the top layer of the compost. When you are potting up ferns or planting them in containers make sure that you leave their crowns exposed and always take great care not to damage the vulnerable fronds. When making arrangements for glass containers such as Wardian cases, arrange the plants first on a piece of card the same size and shape as the container so that you will not need to move them in and out of the container. Cut off any damaged fronds to encourage new ones to grow in their place.

You can divide large ferns when repotting them, and some produce tiny plantlets that can be detached and potted up. You can also grow new ferns from the powdery spores that are produced in little capsules visible as rows of rusty-brown patches, usually on the undersides of the fronds. These grow into a green film of minuscule prothalli from which true ferns develop. The process can take several months, however. Collect spores in a bag tied around a frond and grow them on moist, peaty compost in a seed tray or on a brick in a container of water. Pour boiling water over the compost to sterilize it and powder on the spores, using the tip of a knife. Alternatively, lay a frond spore-side down on the surface. Place the container in a polythene bag and keep it warm and semi-shaded until small plants develop from the green film that appears on the surface. Pot these up and give them more light and constant warmth.

*Left: Adiantum raddianum* (Delta maidenhair fern) has a mass of delicate branching fronds with light green foliage and some people find it easier to grow than other adiantums. The cultivar 'Fragrantissima' has dense and large foliage.
*Right:* A young *Blechnum gibbum* (hard fern) can be kept moist by having its pot plunged into a peat-filled cache pot. This palm-like fern grows into a large specimen and develops a trunk as it ages.

are decoratively crimped and frilled. This and their bright, clear green coloration make a good contrast to smoother and darker foliage.

### Blechnum (hard fern)
These terrestrial ferns are found in sheltered sites in temperate and tropical areas. They need acid soil. *B. chilense* (syn. *B. cordatum*, *B. magellanicum*) has dark green, pinnate fronds, to 1m (3ft) long. It can grow to 1.8m (6ft) high. *B. gibbum* (syn. *Lomaria gibba*) has bright green fronds, to 1m (3ft) long, forming a wide-spreading rosette.

### Cyrtomium falcatum (holly fern)
This unusual plant has glossy, leathery pinnae, shaped like holly leaves. It will grow to 50–60cm (20–24in) high and across and does well in low temperatures and dim light. Provide extra humidity to compensate if temperatures rise to around 21°C (70°) or more.

### Davallia
*D. canariensis* (hare's foot fern, deer's foot fern) has feathery foliage. The sturdy, hairy rhizomes, which grow over the surface of the compost, form part of its attraction. *D. fejeensis* (rabbit's foot fern) has mid-green, finely divided fronds. Grow in medium light with a minimum winter temperature of 10–15°C (50–60°F).

# plant directory

### Adiantum (maidenhair fern)
The evergreen *A. capillus-veneris* (true maidenhair fern) has light green, triangular fronds made up of fan-shaped pinnae. Plants grow to 30cm (12in) high and 40cm (16in) across. *A. raddianum* (syn. *A. cuneatum*; delta maidenhair fern) has black stalks and triangular fronds with rounded pinnae. This is a variable species, which has given rise to many popular cultivars, including the larger 'Fragrantissimum' and 'Lawsoniana', which has sharply triangular fronds.

### Asplenium (spleenwort)
*A. bulbiferum* (mother fern, hen and chicken fern) produces new ferns rather like laying eggs: they grow from small brown bulbils on the fronds and drop off to grow in the soil below. Mature fronds are to 1m (3ft) long and 23cm (9in) wide. The plant likes medium light and average summer temperatures, with a winter minimum of 10°C (50°F). *A. nidus* (bird's nest fern) is an epiphytic plant with bright green fronds to 1m (3ft) long. They are semi-erect and form a broad, spreading funnel. *A. scolopendrium* (syn. *Phyllitis scolopendrium*, *Scolopendrium vulgare*; hart's tongue fern) has irregularly shaped, shuttlecock-like crowns. The fronds are bright green and to 40cm (16in) long. Cultivars in the Crispum Group

*Right:* With its broad, glossy leaves, about 8cm (3in) wide and 45cm (18in) long, *Asplenium nidus* (bird's nest fern) makes an excellent plant for a pot standing alone on a table.
*Below right: Cyrtomium falcatum* 'Rochfordianum' (holly fern) is a dependable fern, which is less susceptible to draughts and dry air than most. Standing the fern's pot in a saucer of wet pebbles provides adequate moisture.

### *Nephrolepis* (sword fern)

The genus contains one of the finest indoor ferns, *N. exaltata* 'Bostoniensis' (Boston fern), which has broad, lance-shaped fronds that arch gracefully. Several other attractive cultivars have been developed, including 'Mini Ruffle', which grows to only 5cm (2in) tall and 8cm (3in) across, and 'Golden Boston' (syn. 'Aurea'), which is similar to 'Bostoniensis' but has golden-yellow fronds. 'Whitmannii' (lace fern) has fronds to 45cm (18in) long with small pinnae. *N. cordifolia* (sword fern, ladder fern) has almost erect fronds to 60cm (2ft) long. The pinnae are sharply toothed. These ferns need bright, indirect light and average summer temperatures, with winter temperatures of 13–16°C (55–61°F).

**Pellaea rotundifolia (button fern)**
This fern from New Zealand has deep green fronds to 30cm (12in) long on wiry stems with button-shaped pinnae. It grows to 25–30cm (10–12in) high and 40cm (16in) across. It needs fairly bright, indirect light, normal summer temperatures and winter temperatures of 10–13°C (50–55°F).

**Platycerium (staghorn fern)**
The genus contains some large ferns. *P. alcicorne* (South American

staghorn) has kidney shaped, mid-green leaves. It can grow to 80cm (32in) high and across. *P. bifurcatum* (which is sometimes sold as *P. alcicorne*; common staghorn fern) is variable but has glossy green fronds that are deeply lobed. It will grow to almost 1m (3ft) tall and about 80cm (32in) across. *P. superbum* (syn. *P. grande* has grey-green, deeply lobed fronds. This is a huge, epiphytic fern, growing to 1.8m (6ft) tall and 1.5m (5ft) across.

**Polystichum (holly fern, shield fern)**
The genus contains species that are perfectly hardy and can be grown in gardens, but in a cool room they can be treated as houseplants. *P. setiferum* (soft shield fern) is a well-known garden fern with dark green fronds forming attractive shuttlecocks. Cultivars in the Actutilobum Group develop tiny plantlets along the upper surface of the fronds. *P. tsussimense* (Tsusina holly fern, Korean rock fern),

*Left*: A larger fern in a pot, such as *Polystichum tsussimense* (Tsusina holly fern), can leave a bare space below it when standing alone on a table. A trailing ivy and a bright blue pot will fill the space.
*Above:* The popular *Platycerium bifurcatum* (staghorn fern) is an epiphyte and grows well without a pot.
*Right:* The variegated *Pteris cretica* var. *albolineata* stands in a white pot with nothing to detract from its slender, rippling fronds.

which is native to China and Japan, has dark green, broad, arching fronds, to 30cm (12in) long, which form a broad shuttlecock. It grows to about 40cm (16in) high and across.

### *Pteris* (brake)

The genus is found in tropical and subtropical forests all over the world. *P. argyraea* (silver brake) is particularly attractive, having a silver-white stripe down the centre of each of the pinnae. The fronds can grow to 60cm (2ft) long, and plants grow to 1m (3ft) high and across. The best known species in the genus is *P. cretica* (brake fern, ribbon fern), which has narrow, ribbon-like pinnae. The pale green fronds grow to about 60cm (2ft) long, and plants can grow to 75cm (30in) high and 60cm (2ft) across. *P. cretica* var. *albolineata* has a broad white line along the centre of each pinna. Several cultivars have been developed from the species, including 'Alexandrae', which has undulating fronds with crested tips, and the compact 'Wimsettii', which has irregularly lobed pinnae.
*P. tremula* (shaking brake, tender brake), which is native to Australia and New Zealand, will eventually grow to 1.5m (5ft) tall and 1m (3ft) across. It has a feathery appearance. All varieties need indirect light with some shade in summer and fairly low temperatures, 10–18°C (50–64°F), in the summer, which should not drop below around 7°C (45°F) in winter.

# bromeliads

The typical houseplant bromeliad is a pineapple-like plant with a rosette of firm, fleshy leaves and, occasionally, an exotic, brightly coloured central flower. Some, similar in form, have an 'urn' or 'vase' at their centre, while a third group, the tillandsias or air plants, have less form and wander rootlessly.

The roots of a bromeliad are used simply for anchoring it to a support, such as the branch of a tree, rather than for getting nourishment from the soil, and the plants flourish when grown in a pot that would be much too small for other plants of the same size. The bolder strap-leaved bromeliads, such as *Ananas* spp. (pineapple), *Aechmea* spp. and *Vriesea* spp., make striking plants grown in pots and also adapt well to hanging baskets.

There are also tillandsias that grow well as specimens in pots and baskets, and the larger grey-leaved tillandsias are good plants for a hanging basket as they have arching foliage, are light and need no watering. Tillandsias are, however, often grown without pots because they can take their nourishment entirely from the surrounding air. Many tillandsias make interesting centrepieces attached to pieces of bark or driftwood or set in large shells and getting food from the air as they do in their native forests. *Cryptanthus* spp. (earth star, starfish plant) and *Fascicularia* spp. are ground-growing air plants, and these can be grown on stones, shells or bark. Cryptanthus are particularly well suited to being grown in open-topped bottles and other glass containers.

*Above*: The leaves of *Neoregelia carolinae* f. *tricolor* are attractively striped in cream, and the whole plant flushes deep pink as it flowers and keeps this colouring for several months.
*Right*: A group of tillandsias, some planted in pebble-covered compost, others attached to bark, looks well in plain pots. Air plants also have an affinity with sea shells. Simple surroundings and hard surfaces suit these plants best.

## CARE AND CULTIVATION

Most of the pineapple-type and vase or urn bromeliads grow in the humid environment of the rain forests of Central and South America, dwelling in dappled light on the branches of trees. Xerophytic bromeliads, such as fascicularia, and cryptanthus (earth stars), are generally ground dwellers that have adapted to the moist air of coastal areas or the inhospitable slopes of high mountain ranges.

Except for tillandsias, most of which do not take to being grown in pots at all, bromeliads for the home should be grown in

Far left: *Ananas comosus* (common pineapple) will eventually bear colourful flowers, but they are principally grown for their striking, spine-edged leaves. *A. comosus* 'Variegatus' has the advantages of a compact form and attractive cream-colour variegation.
Left: The larger, grey-leaved tillandsias are good plants for a hanging basket where the arching foliage can be seen to good effect.

pots that are small for their size, in well-drained fibrous or peaty, preferably lime-free, compost, which has some added charcoal.

Bromeliads must have their specific needs for moisture met. All benefit from frequent misting with tepid, lime-free water, and this is essential for the tillandsias growing without pots. Many bromeliads grown in pots have a rosette of leaves and a central reservoir, and these central vases or urns should be filled with fresh, soft, tepid water, which is emptied and replaced from time to time, but the compost itself should be watered only moderately.

All bromeliads are tropical or subtropical plants that make for dramatic displays. In general they need high humidity and temperatures of 13–15°C (55–60°F), and up to 20°C (70°F) when actively growing in summer. They need warm air,

and a test of this is that the water in the centre of vase and urn types should evaporate away – if it does not, it will become stagnant. In the wild they get their nourishment from organic debris in the air and, in the case of vase and urn types, the detritus that falls into their centres. In the home they should be watered with a balanced fertilizer, diluted to half-strength, every six to eight weeks. This can also occasionally be added to the water with which they are sprayed and to the water in their central reservoirs. Like most flowering plants, bromeliads need to be watered more when flower buds appear and during active growth. To maintain a good level of humidity you can stand the plants on trays of wet pebbles, which can look attractive, or use a mister.

The main attraction of bromeliads is their leaves and

forms, but many also bear beautiful flower spikes, generally consisting of colourful bracts and small, insignificant flowers. Be prepared to wait, because flower spikes normally appear only on mature plants. After flowering the plant may die, but not before it has produced offsets, which can be potted up to make new plants.

# plant directory

### Abromeitiella brevifolia

Formerly known as *A. chlorantha*, which is still sometimes offered as a separate species, these South American bromeliads eventually form large mats, to about 15cm (6in) high, of spiky-leaved rosettes, and they should be grown in large pans rather than in a 'normal' flowerpot. They have tapering, almost triangular leaves ending in a pointed tuft. In summer greenish flowers are borne on mature plants.

### Aechmea

The bromeliads in this genus have strap-shaped leaves that arise from the centre, whey they form a pronounced reservoir. The offsets that grow around the parent plant should be detached when they are about 15cm (6in) high and grown on in small pots. *A. chantinii* (Amazonian zebra plant) has beautifully marked leaves, banded in grey, and edged with spines. The flowerheads are orange-yellow.

The best known species is, perhaps, *A. fasciata* (urn plant, silver vase), which has strong, broad, curving leaves of a dull, bluish-green, marked all over with powdery silver-white. Mature plants have leaves to 50cm (20in) long and 5cm (2in) or more wide and bear a flower spike of pink bracts and tiny, blue flowers. The flowers can last for several months but the plant begins to die after flowering. As long as the air is kept moist the plant will enjoy

*Left:* The bold architectural form and pale blue bloom of the leaves of *Aechmea fasciata* (vase plant) make it a striking plant.
*Right: Ananas comosus* (common pineapple) was introduced and cultivated for its fruit, but is now grown as an ornamental plant.
*Below right: Cryptanthus* spp. (earth stars) have wavy-edged leaves, which may have contrasting bands of colour.

temperatures of up to 26°C (79°F) in summer. It should be kept cooler in winter but not below 15°C (60°F).

The common name of *A. fulgens* (coral berry) is derived from the red berries that follow the blue flowers. It has dark green, spine-edged leaves. It can grow to 50cm (20in) high and 40cm (16in) across. *A. fulgens* var. *discolor* has leaves with purple undersides.

### Ananas  (pineapple)

Pineapples will eventually bear colourful flowers and even, in a warm greenhouse, fruit, but they are principally grown for their striking spine-edged leaves. *A. bracteatus* (red pineapple, wild pineapple) has spiny leaves and, in summer, red and yellow flower spikes. The form 'Tricolor' (syn. *A. bracteatus* 'Striatus') has lovely yellow-striped leaves. *A. comosus*, the pineapple grown commercially, can be grown by cutting off the top of a fruit, leaving it for a couple of days to form a callus and planting in well-drained compost. It will eventually grow to about 1m (3ft) high and 50cm (20in) across. *A. comosus* var. *variegatus* (ivory pineapple) is a compact form with attractive cream-edged leaves. *A. nanus* is similar to *A. comosus* but smaller, growing to about 45cm (18in) high and 60cm (2ft) across.

### Billbergia

Billbergias are especially easy bromeliads to grow. They produce spectacular flowerheads on long, arching stems from the centres of the rosettes, and although each rosette dies after it has flowered, the plant has several at once, in different stages of development. One of the most popular billbergias is *B. nutans* (friendship plant, queen's tears), which has grey-green, sometimes red-tinged, leaves, forming a funnel-shaped rosette. In summer yellow, pink and green flowers, surrounded by red bracts, are borne on arching stems. *B.* x *windii* has mid-green leaves, which are arching and slightly twisted, forming a tubular rosette. Green-yellow flowers with pinkish-red bracts are borne on arching stems in late summer.

### Cryptanthus  (earth star, starfish plant)

Many bromeliads are large, 'stand alone' plants. The earth stars or cryptanthus are small in comparison. There are many species, but all are grown for their striped or banded foliage, arranged in the typical rosette and often with wavy or saw-toothed edges. They produce numerous offsets, and the best way to detach these to form new plants is first to remove the parent plant from its pot and then to pull off the offsets before replanting the parent. Earth stars need normal summer temperatures and a steady 15°C (60°F) in winter. They thrive in glass containers.

*C. bivittatus* is the most popular species. Its leaves have wavy, serrated edges and are 10–15cm (4–6in) long, striped green and pinkish-yellow. *C. bromelioides* also produces spreading rosettes of strap-

shaped, arching leaves, which are finely toothed and wavy edged. *C. bromelioides* var. *tricolor* is larger and has leaves olive green leaves longitudinally striped with white and pink. *C. fosterianus* (pheasant leaf) has ginger-brown leaves brindled in grey, resembling the tail feathers of a pheasant. *C. zonatus* (zebra earth star) has finely toothed, green-brown leaves that are beautifully banded with grey-buff.

### Dyckia

This South American genus contains rosette-forming plants. *D. fosteriana* has attractive silver-grey, toothed leaves, which curve back to form a spreading rosette about 20cm (8in) high and 12cm (5in) across. *D. remotiflora* has dark green leaves, which are edged with hooked spines. Orange flowers appear in late spring. It grows to 30cm (12in) high and 50cm (20in) across.

### Hechtia

These bromeliads are native to the southern United States and Central America. *H. argentea* (syn. *Dyckia argentea*) is a rosette-forming plant with long, tapering leaves, to 60cm (2ft) long, which are silvery-grey and edged with spines. It is a striking plant, growing to 1m (3ft) across and high. *H. epigyna* has bright green leaves, to 45cm (18in) long, which are edged with white teeth and which form rosettes to 60cm (2ft) high and across.

### Neoregelia

The most popular neoregelia is *N. carolinae* (syn. *Aregelia carolinae*, *Nidularium carolinae*). It has mid-green, copper-tinged leaves, which form an open rosette. When plants begin to flower, the centre of the rosette turns red. The leaves of *N. carolinae* f. *tricolor* (blushing bromeliad) are glossy and striped longitudinally in cream and pink. The whole plant blushes red from the centre before it flowers and retains this colouring for several months. The low flowerhead appears at the centre of the rosette.

    *N. spectabilis* (fingernail plant) has red-tipped, green leaves which become purple-brown at the centre. The flue flowers emerge from purple-banded, green bracts.

### Nidularium

*N. fulgens* (syn. *Guzmania picta*), sometimes known as blushing bromeliad, has toothed, bright green leaves that form a spreading rosette to 60cm (2ft) across. The white, purple-blue and red flowers are surrounded by bright red bracts. At the centre of *N. innocentii* (bird's nest bromeliad) is a rosette of short leaves, which turn red before the flowers appear. They are surrounded by longer, broader, green leaves.

### Tillandsia

The species that grow well in pots have long, grassy, rather untidy-looking leaves and spectacular flat, fish- or quill-shaped flowers, made up of overlapping bracts. Many of these are delightful, fairly small plants between 23cm (8in) and 45cm (18in) high. *T. cyanea*, for example, with its vivid-pink flowerhead, is 23cm (9in)

### Fascicularia

These rosette-forming plants are mostly from Chile. *F. bicolor* (syn. *F. andina*) has stiff, spiny toothed leaves to 45cm (18in) long; at flowering time the inner leaves turn bright red. *F. pitcairniifolia* has blue-green, rather glaucous leaves, which can get to 1m (3ft) long. At flowering, the inner circle of leaves turn vivid red around the blue-purple flowerheads.

### Guzmania

The most widely grown species is *G. lingulata* (scarlet star). It has fairly narrow green leaves, to 50cm (20in) long, and eventually produces a flowerhead consisting of flaring red bracts. This is another relatively easy bromeliad, which tolerates a range of normal room temperatures as long as it has plenty of humidity. It should not be fed but its funnel should always have fresh, soft water. It will grow to about 45cm (18in) high and across. *G. sanguinea* produces almost flat rosettes of dark green leaves, to 40cm 916in) long, which become flushed with yellow, red and orange when the plants produces flowers. The flowers themselves are yellow, green or white and are surrounded by vivid red bracts. Plants grow to 20cm (8in) high and about 35cm (14in) across.

high. All tillandsias prefer high summer temperatures of up to 27°C (80°F) and 10–15°C (50–59°F) in winter although they are tough plants and can survive at temperatures as low as 5°C (41°F) as long as the compost is kept only just slightly moist.

Among the tillandsias that can be included in pot-free displays are *T. circinnatoides* (pot-bellied tillandsia), which has spiralling leaf blades, 20–45cm (8–18in) high; *T. ionantha* (blushing bride), 8–10cm (3–4in) high, which has rosettes of silver-grey leaves, flushing red before flowering; *T. geminiflora*, which has bracts of rosy-pink with tiny, violet flowers and grows to 15–20cm (6–8in) high; and *T. ixioides*, which has a narrow, yellow flowerhead and grows to 13cm (5in) high.

*Above left: Vriesea hieroglyphica* (king of bromeliads) forms a rosette of yellow-green leaves irregularly patterned with darker green and purplish on the underside.
*Above: Neoregelia carolinae* 'Flandria' has particularly broad leaves, generously edged and narrowly striped in cream.
*Right: Tillandsia flabellata* is one of the green-leaved tillandsias that are normally grown in a pot. Its leaves are long and tapering and can take on reddish tints.

### Vriesea
These plants, which are closely related to tillandsias, have deeply cupped rosettes of strap-shaped leaves, and many are grown for the attractive leaves alone. *V. fenestralis* has yellowish-green leaves that are speckled with dark green on the upperside and reddish-purple on the underside. Plants can grow to 1m (3ft) high and 50cm (20in) across. *V. hieroglyphica* (king of bromeliads) has purple-marked, yellowish-green leaves that can be up to 60cm (2ft) long and 10cm (4in) wide. The individual rosettes are to 1m (3ft) high and across. *V. splendens* (flaming sword) produces a succession of long-lasting flowerheads of bright red, overlapping bracts on stems 60cm (2ft) high from a rosette of dark green, banded leaves about 40cm (16in) long. The rosette, which forms a central 'cup', dies slowly when the flowering has finished. It needs a temperature of up to 27°C (80°F), with high humidity.

# 6 CACTI & SUCCULENTS

People become addicted to growing cacti, and they are certainly collectable plants and ideal for a sunny windowsill. We associate cacti with the desert, and many do, indeed, grow in the desert regions of Central and South America, but other cacti come from as far north as Canada, and many are native to rainforests. Like bromeliads, many cacti are epiphytes, and the forest-dwelling species grow over forest trees.

Desert-dwelling cacti can survive for long periods without rainfall, getting their moisture from dew or mist and storing nutrients and moisture in their tissues. This is a defining characteristic of succulent plants and it is this capacity that defines cacti as succulents. Botanically, what makes a cactus a cactus is that it has growths, known as areoles. These are cushioned growing points, which are technically compressed lateral branches. Spines, 'wool', flowers and offsets all grow from the areoles. Many succulents resemble cacti in almost every way – even to growing spines – but not in this distinguishing feature. In all but one genus of cactus, *Pereskia*, the plants do not have leaves, but spines or scales.

Because it has leaves, a cactus stores nutrients and water in its body, which consists, botanically, of a stem. The 'bodies' of cacti are generally globular or cylindrical in shape, although opuntias have round, segmented stems, which are flattened, and epiphyllums have stems that look more like strap-shaped leaves, which are again segmented. Many cacti have prominent spines, barbs or bristles, and some have woolly hair. In fact, every cactus has spines even though these may be small and seemingly insignificant. It is not always known or appreciated that all cacti are actually flowering plants, which will flower regularly if well looked after.

The word succulent means juicy, and succulent plants have leaves or stems that are swollen with juices, the stored water and nutrients that enable the plants to survive in harsh conditions all over the world. They normally have a glossy or leathery appearance, and the texture helps to protect them from excessive moisture loss. There is a huge range of succulent plants that can be grown in the home and some of them are among the easiest plants to care for, making them ideal for beginners, for children and for people who have to be away from home a lot. But, as with all plants, you have to understand their nature to grow them successfully.

*Left*: An imaginatively arranged group of cacti makes an absorbing display. Here barrel, columnar and 'lollipop' shapes mingle with two opuntias, which may be recognized by their flattened pads.

*Above*: Displaying related plants in similar pots gives the group added coherence.

*Left*: Many cacti are rounded and attractively ribbed and spined. *Parodia claviceps* has golden spines and quickly forms clusters of spheres topped with patches of white areoles.

*Right above*: *Epiphyllum* 'Reward' is one of the forest cacti that produce beautiful flowers. These rainforest plants hybridize readily and many cultivars have been produced.

*Right below:* A mixed group of small cacti is perfect for a broad, sunny space. Patience is required for the first three or four years, and then many of the cacti will burst into bloom.

plants, such as *Heliocereus speciosus* (sun cactus).

Any large, shallow dish can be used as a container for a cactus garden. Select desert cacti and small succulents for this, so that the plants share similar growing and care requirements. Because these plants all need maximum light, you need to select a container that is the right shape and size to fit in the lightest place that you can offer. Arrange the plants fairly closely to avoid the 'spotted dick' or 'dot' effect – this is an effect caused by groups of plants that have been arranged with little form or structure – and choose a variety of shapes and sizes. A layer of fine grit spread over the compost provides an attractive and suitably dry surface for the cacti, and clean pebbles arranged between the plants completes the effect.

Cacti can look charming in a row, potted in matching pots.

## CARE AND CULTIVATION

From the breathtakingly beautiful, such as *Nopalxochia ackermanii* and the large-flowered epiphyllums (orchid cactus), to the frankly weird and wonderful, such as *Astrophytum asterias* (sea urchin cactus) or the hairy *Cephalocereus senilis* (old man cactus), cacti and succulents make a fine display, and it is a shame that they are not more widely cultivated. This probably stems from their undemanding natures: they will survive almost any treatment except overindulgence. This has resulted in cacti and succulents that are neglected and left to gather dust on people's windowsills at one extreme

and plants that are rotting from overwatering at the other. They need bright light, fresh air and a cool, dry winter rest.

Forest cacti tend to have a trailing habit and large flowers, making them perfect for individual display in hanging baskets, but the interesting shapes and textures of the desert types, and of many succulent plants, can be highlighted by a grouped display where they can be compared and contrasted. A group of small cacti or succulents planted in a single bowl is particularly effective, although larger specimens, such as aloes and agaves, look best in a pot of their own, as can the more curious

Cacti such as mutant cultivars of *Gymnocalycium mihanovichii*, which come with differently coloured heads but are otherwise alike, look best displayed in this simple but attractive way.

Most cacti and succulents need the maximum light possible and are therefore suitable for the sunniest of windowsills. This light-loving characteristic can be exploited to the full by fixing shelves across a sunny window and standing rows of neatly potted cacti on them. You could also arrange the pots in a low-sided basket or a wicker tray. Make sure that the plants are turned frequently so that all parts get equal exposure to the full light. A mixed group of small cacti is perfect for a broad, sunny windowsill.

There is an almost bewildering range of cacti to grow at home, and every garden centre has a fairly wide selection. Some cacti – the forest-growing *Hatiora rosea* (Easter cactus) and *Schlumbergera* x *buckleyi* (Christmas cactus), for example – are sold as seasonal gift plants in department stores, too. It is best to buy cacti that are in flower, because they can take several years to reach maturity and flowering age. Check them carefully, making sure they are sound with no trace of rot or areas that are dry or shrivelled. They should be just the right size for their pot: not too small but not showing signs of roots being cramped. Make sure that they are not exposed to sudden draughts of cold air on their way home. Once you get a taste for cacti you will find that you need to go to a specialist nursery for the more unusual specimens.

*Above: Echinopsis chamaecereus* (peanut cactus) has short stems. The bright red flowers are produced in abundance in spring and summer.
*Left: Astrophytum capricorne* (goat's horn cactus) gets more columnar as it ages and has dark, curled spines (left). *A. myriostigma* (bishop's cap) is covered in silvery-white scales (right).
*Opposite: Cereus. uruguayanus* typifies desert cacti with its spines and well-defined shape.

# desert cacti

Desert cacti must have well-drained compost. Special cactus compost, or any potting compost to which added sharp sand or gravel has been added, can be used. The cacti should be well watered with tepid water in spring and summer, but the compost should be allowed to become almost completely dry between waterings. In winter they should be kept almost completely dry, especially if they are in cool conditions. Cacti should be fed about every three weeks during periods of active growth, with well-diluted tomato plant fertilizer.

Most desert cacti do best if kept in winter temperatures of 10–13°C (50–55°F) but can withstand temperatures as low as 5°C (41°F). Repot only when the roots absolutely fill the pot.

# plant directory

### Astrophytum
These slow-growing cacti come from the southern United States and Mexico. *A. asterias* (syn. *Echinocactus asterias*; sand dollar cactus, sea urchin cactus) is hemispherical, growing to 10cm (4in) high and across, with six to ten almost flat ribs. Yellow flowers with red throats are borne in summer. *A. myriostigma* (syn. *Echinocactus myriostigma*; bishop's cap cactus) has ribbed sides, gathered up in the shape of a bishop's mitre. It is smooth and greyish-green, speckled with white, and the four to eight ribs are marked with white, felty blobs (areoles); it eventually grows to about 23cm (9in) high and to 30cm (12in) across. When four or five years old it produces a succession of scented, lemon-yellow flowers in summer. Astrophytums grow best in a light, sunny position and should be fed once every two weeks in summer with tomato fertilizer.

### Cephalocereus
The three cacti now included in the genus are from Mexico. They all columnar and have numerous spines. The best known species is *C. senilis* (old man cactus), which will grow to 12m (40ft) tall in the desert but is extremely slow growing. Young plants have 12–15 ribs, and the yellow spines are produced from closely set areoles, which produce 20–30 soft, white hairs. These hairs, which give the cactus its appearance, can be 13cm (5in) long. In summer nocturnal pink flowers are borne. Eventually, at home, the beards need to be washed with detergent; this should be done outside on a warm, dry day.

### Cereus
The genus contains tree-like cacti from South America and the Caribbean. *C. uruguayanus* (syn. *C. peruvianus*; Peruvian cereus) can grow to 90cm (3ft) fairly quickly in a warm, sunny room. Its columns are blue-green, ribbed and spined. Under the name *C. uruguayanus* 'Monstrosus' (or 'Monstruosus') a number of mutations with gargoyle-like side branches are sold.

### Cleistocactus
These cacti from mountainous areas of South America have tall, slender stems, with the narrow ribs ornamented by neat spines and woolly areoles. One or two forms are branched or trailing. *C. strausii* (silver torch), which has silvery-white spines that are covered with fine bristles and grows to about 1m (3ft) high and across.

### Echinocactus
These slow-growing cacti originate in the southern United States and Mexico. *E. grusonii* (golden barrel cactus, mother-in-law's cushion) is a popular non-flowering cactus. It has sharp golden-yellow spines and a deeply ribbed stem, ultimately 60cm (2ft) high and 80cm (32in) across, which is topped with a depression and a crown of yellow hairs.

and often barbed spines. *F. latispinus* is bright green, with 15–23 ribs and pinkish-yellow coloured spines. It is slow growing, eventually getting to 40cm (16in) high and across, and in summer has red, white, purple or yellow flowers.

### Gymnocalycium
There are more than 50 species in the genus, and they are found throughout South America. *G. bruchii* (syn. *G. lafadense*) forms clumps of dark green stems with 12 ribs and each to about 4cm (1½in) high. In summer pink flowers are borne. *G. mihanovichii* is a globular cactus with a grey-green stem and eight prominent ribs. It has given rise to a number of mutant forms that lack chlorophyll and that are grafted on to robust plants of *Hylocereus*. These plants grow to about 13cm (5in) tall.

### Heliocereus
The cacti in this genus are native to Central America. They vary widely in habit and appearance, some being more or less erect, while others are trailing. *H. cinnabarinus* is a trailing

### Echinopsis
The common name of the much re-named *Echinopsis chamaecereus* (syn. *Cereus silvestrii*, *Chamaecereus silvestrii*, *Lobivia silvestrii*; peanut cactus, gherkin cactus) is derived from its rather marrow-shaped stems, each to about 10cm (4in) tall, which look like bristle-covered gherkins or peanut pods. It is fast growing and produces red or deep orange flowers in late spring. Several hybrids are available but these are less fast growing. It should be brought out of its winter rest in early spring.

### Espostoa
The genus includes ten species of columnar cacti, which are slow growing, eventually tree-like. *E. lanata* (snowball cactus) is columnar, with 20–30 ribs, and in the wild it grows to 1.5m (5ft) or more. White or yellowish hairs emerge from the areoles, giving the plant its common name. *E. melanostele* has a grey-green stem, covered with brown areoles. Plants will grow to 1.8m (6ft) in the wild. In summer white, yellow or brown flowers are produced.

### Ferocactus
Native to southern parts of the United States and to Mexico and Guatemala, these cacti are usually solitary. They are mostly spherical in shape and can very slowly reach 60cm (2ft) or more in height. They have ferocious, stiff,

cactus, with dark green stems with white, yellow or brown spines. In summer it bears bright red flowers. *H. speciousus* (syn. *Cereus speciosus*) is semi-erect, with branched, green stems that have three to five ribs. The small spines are white or brown and the carmine flowers are borne during the summer.

### Mammillaria
The genus includes the most popular and widely available of all cactus species, of which there are more than a hundred. They form cushions, mounds – some cylindrical – and 'cauliflower' heads, all covered in numerous tiny spines. In spring they bear either a few large flowers or more smaller ones, which are followed by fruits. But beware: many mammillarias also have vicious hooks. *M. longimamma* (syn. *Dolichothele longimamma*) is a small, long-lived cactus with several narrow, fleshy projections, each of which has a lightly spined tip. In summer this plant produces shiny, bright yellow, upright, bell-shaped flowers that have many petals.

### Opuntia (prickly pear)
Most opuntias are the multiple-lollipop type, with flattened stems that grow in rounded segments. Among those species popular as houseplants are

*O. brasiliensis*, which makes a large plant that grows to 6m (20ft) or more high; *O. microdasys* (bunny ears) has round, golden-tufted pads; and *O. microdasys* var. *rufida* (syn. *O. rufida*; red bunny ears), which has brownish-red tufts and grows to about 60cm (2ft) high and across. *O. subulata* (awl cactus) is unusual in that it has cylindrical, many-branched stems that are covered in projecting awl-shaped, green leaves and yellowish-spined areoles. Although this plant grows to 3m (10ft) in the wild it is seldom taller than 75cm (30cm) in the home.

### Oreocereus
Formerly known as *Borzicactus*, this genus contains cacti that come from mountainous areas in South America. *O. aurantiacus* (syn. *Borzicactus aurantiacus*, *Matucana aurantiaca*), which grows to about 15cm (6in) high and across, has a slightly flattened globe shape, and bright orange-yellow flowers sprout from the top of the stem in summer. Bright light, and fairly generous watering and fortnightly feeding in summer encourage flowering.

### Parodia
The genus contains cacti that were previously classified as *Eriocactus*, *Notocactus* and *Wigginsia*. They are

mostly small, taking ten years to reach up to 18cm (7in), and are generally spherical and spiny, some becoming cylindrical as they age. The flowers, which can sometimes be disproportionately large, are produced on the top of the 'ball'. *P. leninghausii* (syn. *Eriocactus leninghausii*; golden ball cactus) grows to 60cm (2ft) but only about 20cm (8in) across, and is liked for its golden spines. *P. ottonis* (syn. *Notocactus ottonis* is a typical small ball cactus, which has a mass of yellow flowers in spring. Ball cacti are easily grown from seed.

### Rebutia
This genus now also includes plants that used to be known as *Sulcorebutia* and *Weingartia*. These small cacti are perhaps the easiest to grow. They are often known as crown cacti, a common name that describes the way flowers often form a ring around the base of the plant. They have funnelled, many-petalled flowers and form mounds 10–15cm (4–6in) high. *R. aureiflora* is studded in late spring with yellow flowers; *R. minuscula* (syn. *R. violaciflora*) comes in forms with red or violet flowers; *R. senilis* has flowers in red, yellow or lilac in late spring and early summer. Rebutias may die quite soon after flowering, but they produce offsets from which replacement plants can be grown.

*Left: Aporocactus flagelliformis* (rat-tail cactus) makes an ideal plant for a medium hanging pot.
*Above: Nopalxochia ackermanii* flowers very prolifically, especially if not repotted for several years.
*Above right: Hatiora gaertneri* is the red-flowered 'Easter cactus'.

# forest cacti

Forest cacti are very different from desert cacti. They usually have spectacularly beautiful hanging flowers growing from the tips of segmented stems, which look like chains of fleshy leaves. They grow in a trailing manner because of their habit of growing over trees. Because of this habit they are used to dappled shade, although, being tropical and subtropical plants, they need quite bright light; they should be kept in good light but protected from strong sun. Like all rainforest plants they need light, lime-free, well-drained compost and high humidity, and they should be frequently misted with tepid, soft water. These cacti should be rested in a cool place at a temperature of 10–13°C (50–55°F) after flowering and watered sparingly until flower buds appear; then water them moderately and feed weekly with a fairly weak solution of balanced fertilizer and move them to a position that has higher temperatures.

# plant directory

### Aporocactus
These epiphytic cacti from Mexico are trailing plants, grown for the slender stems and colourful flowers. *A. flagelliformsi* (syn. *Cereus flagelliformis*) has grey-green stems with 10–14 ribs and red-brown spines. Each stem can grow to 1.8m (6ft) long. Bright pink flowers are borne in spring.

### Epiphyllum (orchid cactus)
Epiphyllums are forest cacti: rainforest plants that, in summer, produce some of the most beautiful of all flowers. They cross-breed readily, and many hybrids have now been bred to be grown as houseplants, including 'Reward', which has yellow flowers, and 'Cambodia', which has purplish-red flowers with ruffled petals. Epiphyllum flowers are usually about 10–15cm (4–6in) wide. Some epiphyllums have been reclassified in *Nopalxochia*.

### Hatiora
Formerly known as *Rhipsalidopsis*, the genus contains the well-known Easter cactus, *H. rosea* (syn. *Rhipsalidopsis rosea*), a shrubby plant with flat, green segments and, in the early spring, vivid pink flowers. *H. gaertneri* (syn. *Rhipsalidopsis gaertneri*, *Schlumbergera gaertneri*), which is also sometimes called the Easter cactus, is a spreading plant with leaf-like stems. Bright red, funnel-shaped flowers are produced during the spring.

### Nopalxochia
Many of the plants now classified in this genus were formerly known as epiphyllums, including *N. ackermannii* (syn. *Epiphyllum ackermannii*), which is an erect plant with flat, fleshy stems. In late spring to early summer it bears orange-red flowers. There are now many named cultivars (still sometimes named as epiphyllums),

including 'Celestine', which has pale pink-red flowers, 'Jennifer Ann', which has yellow flowers, and 'Moonlight Sonata', which has purplish-pink flowers.

### Schlumbergera (Christmas cactus)
The genus is closely allied to *Hatiora* and is sometimes also known as *Zygocactus*. However, most of the plants offered for sale are cultivars that are grown for their reliable and colourful flowers. They have the typical, segmented, flattened stems and make spreading plants, suitable for a hanging basket, although they are enormously dull when not in flower. There are many named forms to choose from, including 'Gold Charm', which has yellow flowers, 'Joanne', which has red and purple flowers, and 'Weinachtesfreude', which has pale and dark red and purple flowers.

# succulents

Apart from the cacti, there are 50 or more families of plants that can be classified as succulents. The cacti are in origin confined almost exclusively to the Americas, but the rest of the succulents come also from Africa and parts of Europe. Like the desert cacti they are dry land plants (many of them grow side by side with cacti), and nearly all have the same needs for plentiful sun and a free-draining compost. The need to be watered freely in summer but only when the compost has become nearly dry, and during winter water should be reduced and they should be kept at temperatures around 10°C (50°F).

In summer most succulents need some well-diluted fertilizer every three to four weeks and fresh air rather than humidity. Some succulents store water and nutrients in their swollen, fleshy leaves (the leaf succulents), others, the stem succulents, have tough, fleshy stems; a third kind, the root succulents, have swollen roots of various kinds in which their reserves of water are stored.

Left: *Aloe aristata* has orange-pink flowers on tall stems, which spring from dense rosettes of sharply pointed, white-edged leaves. The rosette is only 10–15cm (4–6in) high, with the flower stems 30cm (12in) high.
Right: *Agave americana* 'Marginata' has the characteristic broad, wavy leaves, which in this variety are edged and narrowly striped with creamy-yellow.

# plant directory

### Adenia
These plants come from Africa, Madagascar and Burma, and the tiny flowers are followed by yellow, green or red fruits. *A. digitata* (syn. *A. buchananii*, *Modecca digitata*) grows from a caudex (swollen root), which can get to 30cm (12in) across. The dark green leaves are borne in a cluster on top of the caudex. Yellow flowers are followed by red fruits. *A. spinosa* has a huge caudex, 1.8m (6ft) across and spiny branches. White flowers are followed by yellow fruit.

### Adenium obesum (desert rose, impala lily)
This variable, caudex-forming plant comes from Africa and the Arabian peninsula. It is also known as *A. arabicum*, *A. micranthum*, *A. speciosum* and *Nerium obesum*. The bottle-shaped caudex, up to 1m (3ft) long, is topped by brown stems and grey-green leaves. Red, pink or white flowers are borne in summer. Plants can reach 1.5m (5ft) in height.

### Agave
These rosette-forming plants from the Americas include many popular houseplants, although some species are potentially large and are best grown in a cool greenhouse. *A. utahensis* has grey-green leaves with spines along the wavy margins. It grows to 30cm (12in) high but spreads indefinitely. *A. victoriae-reginae* (syn. *A. consideranti*) is perhaps the favourite as a houseplant. The many dark green, spine-tipped leaves are neatly edged with white, and plants eventually grow to 50cm (20in) high and across.

### Aloe
Aloes have rosettes of stiff, leathery, tooth-edged leaves, broad at the base and tapering to a point. The leaves are often blotched, striped, banded or striated. The flowers are bell-shaped – generally orange – and grow in cones on tall, erect stems. There are small aloes, such as *A. humilis* (hedgehog aloe), with bluish, white-toothed leaves and growing to 10cm (4in) high, and *A. aristata* (*A. ellenbergeri*; brush aloe, lace aloe), which has white-spotted leaves and reaches some 10–15cm (4–6in) high. Medium-sized species include the 30cm (12in) high *A. variegata* (syn. *A. ausana*, *A. punctata*; partridge-breasted aloe) with its white-patterned leaves. One of the giant species is *A. arborescens* (tree aloe), which can easily grow to 1m (3ft) in a container.

### Cotyledon
These African succulents have fleshy leaves borne in opposite pairs. *C. orbiculata* grows to 60cm (2ft). It has white-grey leaves covered with waxy white bloom and edged with red. *C. orbiculata* var. *oblonga* (syn. *C. undulata*; silver crown) has red-edged leaves, like fleshy cabbage leaves, with undulating margins.

### Crassula
There are many crassulas, generally with small, rounded or sometimes triangular leaves and succulent, sometimes twisting stems. One of the best known species is *C. ovata* (syn. *C. arborescens*, *C. argentea*; jade plant, money tree) It looks like a tiny, exotic tree with a sturdy, fleshy stem and equally fleshy deep green, waxy leaves. It can grow to 1.8m (6ft) tall but is usually less in a container. The cactus-like *C. muscosa* (syn. *C. lycopodioides*; rat tail plant, lizard tail) shows how different plants of the same genus can be. It has upright branching stems in light green, completely covered in little triangular, fleshy leaves from top to bottom.

### Echeveria
This is another rosette-forming group of plants from southern United States and Central America. *E. derenbergii* (painted lady) has rosettes of piled-up fleshy leaves with blue bloom and orange flowers on towering stems. It grows to 10cm (4in) high to about 30cm (12in) across. *E. elegans* has pale blue-green leaves forming small rosettes, to 5cm (2in) high and forming clumps to 30cm (12in) across.

### Euphorbia

This large genus contains plants that are suitable for the garden as well as for growing as houseplants. *E. obesa* (living baseball) is a cactus-like pincushion with grey and yellow gingham marking and crimped ridging. It grows to 15cm (6in) high and 13cm (5in) across.

### Gasteria

These clump-forming succulents from southern Africa have fleshy leaves arranged in tiers. *G. carinata* var. *verrucosa* (syn. *G. verrucosa*; ox tongue) has grey-green, tapering leaves, which have thick margins and are covered in white tubercles (warts). Each rosette of leaves grows to 15cm (6in) high and to 30cm (12in) across. *G. obliqua* (syn. *G. pulchra*) has almost triangular, grey-green leaves with white margins. Plants are to 30cm (12in) high and 45cm (18in) across.

### Haworthia

Haworthias have strong, rather plump, broad tapering leaves, which grow from small stems in packed rosettes and are often said to be 'warty'. *H. pumila* (syn. *H. margaritifera*; pearl plant) has such dense rosettes that they are almost spherical and the leaves are encrusted with decorative pearly 'warts'. *H. retusa* is a rosette-forming succulent, with fleshy leaves to 5cm (2in) long.

### Kalanchoe

The genus is best known for the hybrids of *K. blossfeldiana* (flaming Katy), which have red, orange, yellow and pink flowers. Among the other species are *K. daigremontiana* (syn. *Bryophyllum daigremontianum*; Mexican hat plant), which has green leaves spotted with red. Adventitious plantlets form around the edges of the leaves and can be potted up. *K. fedtschenkoi* is an upright succulent with blue-green leaves with boldly scalloped edges.

### Kleinia

The plants are related to the familiar garden genus *Senecio* but look quite different. *K. stapeliiformis* (syn.

*Far left:* The broad yellow margins of *Sanseveria trifasciata* 'Laurentii' (mother-in-law's tongue) help the plant to make a bold statement against a plain background.
*Left:* The many euphorbias have no one distinctive form. The remarkable *Euphorbia obesa* (living baseball, gingham golfball) is dome shaped, but other euphorbias have branching, tree-like stems.
*Left below:* The bright green leaves of *Sedum morganianum* (donkey's tail) are easily detached, so care must be taken when handling these plants.
*Right: Kalanchoe blossfeldiana* (flaming Katy) can be bought in flower at any time. Red, orange, pink, yellow and white cultivars are available.

*Senecio stapeliiformis*) is an erect plant with fleshy, glaucous green stems with dark green longitudinal lines. Red-orange flowerheads are produced in summer.

### Lithops (living stones)
These dwarf succulents from southern Africa consist of two opposing 'bodies' topped with large, daisy-like flowers. *L. marmorata* has pale grey bodies and scented white flowers. *L. turbiniformis* (syn. *L. hookeri*) has brown-grey bodies and red and yellow flowers.

### Pachyphytum
These rosette-forming perennials from Mexico have fleshy, swollen leaves. *P. longifolium* has glaucous blue leaves, which are elongated at the tips. Racemes of flowers are borne in spring. *P. oviferum* (sugar almond plant) has pale green-grey leaves tinged with blue. The rosettes grow up to 13cm (5in) tall and as much as 30cm (12in) across.

### Sansevieria
The genus includes the well-known *S. trifasciata* (mother-in-law's tongue) from western Africa, which has sword-shaped, upright leaves, to 1.02m (4ft) tall. The leaves are banded and marbled. 'Golden Hahnii' and 'Silver Hahnii' are dwarf forms; 'Laurentii' has leaves with broad yellow margins.

### Sedum
As well the many sedums that will grow in the garden, there are several species that can be grown as houseplants. Some have fleshy and some have cylindrical 'jelly bean' leaves. Many of them have branching, prostrate stems. *S. morganianum* (donkey's tail, burro's tail) comes from Mexico and has stems that can trail as much as 1m (3ft). It makes an ideal plant for a hanging basket, sometimes bearing clusters of pink flowers at the ends throughout the summer. These stems are crowded with bright green leaves. In the similar *S. sieboldii* 'Mediovariegatum', which comes from Japan, the leaves are a pink-patterned, cool blue-grey.

# 7 BULBS

Many of the best loved indoor flowering plants are grown from bulbs, corms (technically stems) or tubers (underground storage organs). Most of all we associate bulbs with spring, and some of the long-time favourites are spring-flowering, with early indoor hyacinths, crocuses, daffodils and other forms of narcissi and tulips reminding us that winter is coming to an end. Specially prepared bulbs make spring narcissi and hyacinths available for Christmas in the northern hemisphere, a long time before they will be flowering in parks and gardens. But bulbs, corms and tubers can produce lovely flowers at all times of year.

*Left*: Whatever colour hyacinth you choose, their heady fragrance will bring a breath of spring to any winter room.

if you do not grow them yourself. This is really simple, and bringing your own bulbs into flower provides an extra thrill, as well as saving money and giving you a much wider choice of plants.

You can just wander into your local garden centre at the last minute to see what they have in stock; or you may find yourself buying bulbs on impulse without even knowing what you plan to do with them. But sending for the catalogues of the major bulb producers and selecting and ordering bulbs in good time can become a pleasant ritual. If you order from a reputable supplier you can be guaranteed good bulbs in perfect condition. If you buy from retailers, go early in the season (late summer for the majority of spring bulbs) to get the best choice and the freshest bulbs.

Select bulbs or corms that are firm and of good size for the type of plant, and that feel heavy for their size. Make sure that they show no sign of mould, damp or damage. Remember to check that bulbs for early indoor flowering have been specially prepared for 'forcing'.

Bulb fibre (which is made up of peat or coir fibre, mixed with crushed oyster shells and charcoal) is light, convenient and cheaper than potting compost. If you do not intend to keep your bulbs after their first flowering it is an adequate growing medium, but it contains no nutrients and is intended for short-term use only. Soil-based potting compost contains a balanced mix of nutrients and is more akin in structure to the bulbs' natural growing medium, enabling bulbs to develop and replenish themselves after flowering, and

is more suitable for bulbs that are to be grown on in future years.

When you buy bulbs, get the bulb fibre or compost for planting them in, the pots and anything else you will need, such as charcoal to add to the compost if you are using pots without drainage. Plant the bulbs without delay so that they do not have a chance to deteriorate through being stored, and to get them off to an early start.

Always give careful consideration to the pot or container for indoor displays because this can make or mar the effect you are hoping to create. Hyacinths, daffodils and the other narcissi, tulips and crocuses are normally grown in bowls that have no drainage, and although simple and practical plastic bowls are sold for this purpose, an attractive china, glazed earthenware or terracotta pot is much more suitable. The container should be wide and shallow, and preferably non-porous, because if it is of porous material (as are most terracotta pots), its damp base will damage table tops and other surfaces. The remedy is to place a saucer or plate under it, which can spoil the effect, or to stand porous containers on a tiled windowsill or kitchen top.

Larger bulbs, such as the various lilies that are grown as individual specimens, are usually best grown in standard flowerpots that are stood in saucers; there is a good choice of ornamental versions of these. Ordinary clay pots can also be used, but plastic pots are always best hidden by a decorative container that suits both the flower and the room.

It is usually best to consign all hardy bulbs that have been grown indoors to the garden after they have flowered because they cannot be relied upon to give a good repeat performance, but there is really no reason for not keeping most tender indoor bulbs, such as amaryllis, begonia tubers and cyclamen corms, for indoor flowering the following year. If they are correctly treated they should perform indoors year after year.

A pot of bulbs in flower is a visual delight in its own right, but a large part of the pleasure is lost

# daffodils

Probably the favourite among the bulbs grown for indoor flowers are daffodils (and other popular narcissi), and there is such a wide range that it would be possible to have different types in flower from early winter until well into the spring.

Daffodils belong to the *Narcissus* genus, and the word daffodil, although used loosely to describe all narcissi, is used more specifically for those flowers that have prominent trumpets and a single bloom on each stem. We usually think of them as being yellow, but there are white and cream cultivars. The other members of the genus have cups and trumpets of varying sizes, some have several flowers on each stem, some are highly scented, and some have double flowers.

If you want an early performance from all bulbs, not just narcissi, you must make sure that you use bulbs that have been prepared for forcing, because they will have been artificially subjected to a cold 'winter' period and can be made ready to begin growing indoors

*Left*: Hardy daffodils make a good show indoors. Tall cultivars, such as 'King Alfred' and 'Dutch Master', or shorter stemmed varieties, such as 'Tête-à-Tête' and 'February Gold', grow well as houseplants. *Right*: Bright yellow daffodils are symbolic of spring, and an indoor display is at its best when the bulbs are planted close together.

## INDOOR PLANTING

much earlier than normal. They can be brought into flower especially early or introduced gradually to warmth so that they are only just ahead of their natural seasons. Ordinary, unprepared bulbs can be used if you do not want an unnaturally early show.

Small and miniature narcissi, such as 'February Gold' and 'Tête-à-Tête', are among the best for growing early indoors. Bulbs planted in late summer can be brought into good light in winter for Christmas flowering (in the northern hemisphere). For scented flowers grow *N. papyraceus* (syn. *N.* 'Paper White'; paper white narcissus), which has as many as ten intensely fragrant, gleaming white flowers on each stem. These narcissi can also be forced in glass containers of water and pebbles, with a little charcoal added to keep the water sweet.

**1** Plant daffodils in late summer using one cultivar per bowl. Half-fill a clean bowl with damp, sterilized compost or bulb fibre.

**2** Check the height of the compost, using a bulb to measure. When planted the tops of the bulbs should be just about level with the rim of the bowl. Space the bulbs in the bowl so that they are close together but are not quite touching. A full bowl will give the best display with a host of flowers.

**3** Starting from the middle, add more compost or fibre, pushing it gently between the bulbs. Fill the bowl to within 1cm (½in) of the rim. If the bowl has drainage holes, water it well and allow to drain. Otherwise water lightly.

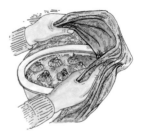

**4** Wrap the bowl in polythene and keep in a cool spot. Check regularly to see that the compost is still damp: water if not. Bring the bowl indoors and gradually increase warmth when the shoots are 5cm (2in) high.

# crocuses & tulips

After narcissi, crocuses and tulips are the most popular spring bulbs. As with naricssi, many cultivars have been developed, and there are now flowers in every imaginable shade and many new shades.

When you are choosing tulip species to force for winter flowering indoors, bear in mind that you should pick early types that will cope with a certain degree of warmth as these are more likely to get good results.

The best place to keep tulips and crocuses once they have begun to flower is in a relatively cool room, away from radiators or fires, as they will soon cease flowering, wilt and die off if kept in a warm, dry atmosphere.

## Forcing tulips

Plant tulips in late summer or early autumn for indoor flowering. Early tulips, both single and double forms, are the best types for growing indoors. To help their roots to form quickly you can peel off the outer brown skin. Keep the pots in the coldest part of the garden, covered with a thick layer of soil topped with black polythene, or in the coolest, darkest place you can provide. Check every ten days or so to make sure the compost is still damp. Bring the pots into a warm room in early winter but keep them in dim light. When there is about 10cm (4in) growth, give the tulips full light and a temperature of about 20°C (68°F). They should then flower around Christmas (in the northern hemisphere). Introduce them only gradually to warmth and light for later flowering.

## Crocus pots

Spring-flowering crocuses are among the earliest flowers to appear in the garden, and corms bought for forcing will bring a splash of colour indoors even earlier. Crocuses planted in autumn open their goblet-like flowers in late winter or early spring. Most spring-flowering crocuses are hybrids of C. chrysanthus, and they are available in a wide range of colours, from the silvery pale blue of 'Blue Pearl' to the dramatic yellow and purple-striped 'Gipsy Girl'.

It is possible to obtain special containers with holes in the sides, and these are perfect for crocuses. Soak the pot for 24 hours, then put a layer of clay pellets or other drainage material in the bottom of the pot. Put in some damp compost or bulb fibre and position the corms into the holes from the inside, so that their 'noses' are just sticking out on the outside. Firm in, adding more compost as necessary to fill the pot. Add more corms at the top. Cover to keep out the light, taking care not to damage the 'noses'.

*Opposite left*: Crocus corms are usually sold by cultivar name and are available in many shades of cream and yellow, blue and purple, as well as white.
*Opposite right:* Indispensable for brightening up garden borders in early and mid-spring, tulips will also add colour and cheer to any room in the house.
*Above left:* The bright red tulip 'Red Riding Hood' has attractive maroon or purple-brown markings on the leaves.
*Above:* The vibrant hues and strong forms of tulips make them popular indoor bulbs.

# hyacinths

Cultivars developed from *Hyancinthus orientalis* are the most popular indoor hyacinths, with fragrant flowers in white and shades of pink, blue, yellow and red. New cultivars are appearing all the time, some with double flowers, but 'Carnegie' (pure white flowers), 'City of Haarlem' (cream-coloured flowers), 'Hollyhock' (bright red, double flowers), 'Ostara' (blue flowers) and 'Sheila' (pale pink flowers) have stood the test of time.

Plant the bulbs from late summer to early autumn, keeping bulbs of the same cultivar in one pot. For a good show, the bowl should be just large enough to allow a little space between the bulbs. After flowering, hyacinths can be planted in the garden, and they will flower in subsequent years. Over time, however, the flower spikes will become less dense.

## PLANTING HYACINTH BULBS

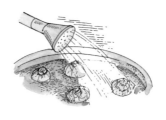

**1** Make sure the pot is clean, to prevent the risk of mould and infection, and half-fill it with damp potting compost or bulb fibre. Position the bulbs on the surface of the compost. If you are using an odd number of bulbs, start with one central bulb and arrange the rest around it.

**2** Seat the bulbs in the compost, with a gap of 1cm (½in) between them. Add more compost – to within 1cm (½in) of the rim – and leave the bulb tops showing. Firm the compost gently. Water pots with drainage thoroughly and allow to drain; water pots without drainage sparingly.

**3** Store, wrapped in black polythene, in a cool place such as a shed, cellar or cupboard in an unheated room. Check occasionally that the compost is still moist and water if necessary. Bring the pot into a cool room when when the shoots reach 5–8cm (2–3in) high.

*Left*: The heavily scented flowerheads of *Hyacinthus orientalis* (Dutch hyacinths) are one of the pleasures of late winter and spring.
*Right:* A bulb glass makes a lovely container for a single hyacinth. The bulb sits neatly within the rim, and its white, fleshy roots fill the rest of the glass, so that the whole plant is visible.
*Below:* Even one hyacinth can brighten up a whole room.

## Using a Bulb Glass

*Hyacinths are the best plants for a bulb glass. They should be started off in late summer or early autumn, using bulbs that have been prepared for forcing. Fill the glass up to the neck with water and sit the bulb in the container with its base just in the water. Keep the glass in a cool, dark place until the leaves begin to show, when the roots should be 8–10cm (3–4in) long, then bring it into the warmth and light in gentle stages. Keep the water level topped up so that the bulb base is just in the water, especially until the hyacinth's roots have developed.*

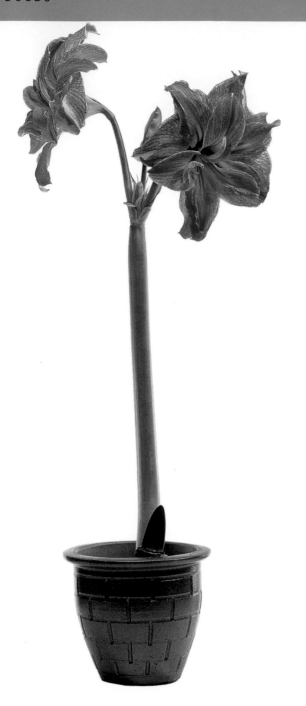

range in colour from beautiful deep red to the palest of pinks, and double flowers, flowers with frilled petals and even striped flowers are increasingly available. Hippeastrums will produce between two and six flowers on each stem.

Use a soil-based compost for the large bulbs, which should be planted so that the neck and shoulders are above the compost. Water sparingly but never let the compost dry out completely until a shoot emerges from the bulb. Increase the amount of water given and feed the plants once a week with a balanced liquid fertilizer diluted to half strength. Position the plants in good light but not direct sun. After flowering has finished gradually reduce the amount of water while the leaves die back. The bulbs should be kept completely dry during their dormant period and then brought back into growth in late autumn for early spring flowering.

Hippeastrums do not respond well to having their roots disturbed at all, and they grow perfectly well in pots that would appear to be too small for the large bulbs. After three to four years, however, bulbs should be potted up. This should be done in autumn before they are brought into growth again to avoid stressing the plant.

New cultivars are appearing every year, but reliable favourites include 'Apple Blossom', which has white flowers shading to a delicate pink at the edges, 'Picotee', which white flowers finely edged in red, 'Red Lion', which has scarlet flowers, and the double-flowered 'Lady Jane', which has pink and white striped flowers.

# hippeastrums

These exotic looking flowers – usually (though incorrectly) known as amaryllis – are increasingly popular houseplants, bearing their huge, showy flowers on erect stems above the strap-shaped leaves in winter and early spring. The funnel-shaped flowers, which can reach as much as 15cm (6in) across,

*Opposite*: With care and summer dormancy, hippeastrums can be brought into flower for several seasons.
*Left:* In order to force a *Clivia miniata* (Kaffir lily) to flower this well, it must be given a resting period and very little water until the flower stalk is at least 15cm (6in) long.

# tender bulbs

While hardy bulbs – narcissi, tulips, hyacinths, crocuses and the like – can be grown outside in temperate climates and can be persuaded to flower indoors in late winter and early spring, there are many tender bulbs that can be grown as houseplants and that will flower at various times of the year. Unlike the hardy bulbs, these plants do not need to be forced.

Pot them in soil-based compost in pots with good drainage and keep them in the light at normal temperatures. Water fairly sparingly until shoots appear and then increasingly generously. All but the evergreen tender bulbs need an annual rest. After they have flowered continue watering until the leaves and flower stems have died down, then cut them off at the base. Store the bulbs – either in their pots or in a box of peat – in a cool, frost-free, dark place without watering. Bring into a warm room and begin to water again in the planting season.

*Left:* Commonly known as Kaffir lilies, clivias will flower year after year if given a cool winter rest. The pot should not be moved once the plant is in bud or while it is flowering and the plant should not be repotted.

*Right:* Bulbous irises can all be grown indoors, and the reticulatas make particularly lovely, softly scented, spring-flowering houseplants. The many named cultivars in this group are mainly in shades of blue.

*Far right:* Lilies make excellent pot plants. They can be persuaded to flower at any time of year, depending on when they are planted, as long as they are kept cold before planting.

# plant directory

### *Babiana stricta* (baboon root)
This cormous species is native to South Africa and requires a minimum winter temperature of 5°C (41°F). It has upright stems and leaves, with small, scented flowers growing up the stems in spring. The funnel- to tubular-shaped flowers may be purple, mauve, blue or, occasionally, yellow, and plants grow to 15–30cm (6–12in) high. Flowering and planting times can be varied, but corms that are planted in the spring will flower in the following autumn. Among the available cultivars are 'Purple Star' and 'Tubergen's Blue'.

### *Clivia miniata* (Kaffir lily)
This is an evergreen perennial from South Africa, which needs a farily warm minimum winter temperature of 10°C (50°F). It is not technically a bulb but develops a swollen, bulb-like base. Plants grow up to 45cm (18in) tall and from late spring to summer produce flaring, tubular flowers in orange, light red or cream on a sturdy stem that is surrounded by strap-shaped, glossy, green leaves. Plant them in spring. Clivias do not like their roots to be disturbed and do best when their root growth is slightly restricted, making them excellent container plants.

### *Freesia* cvs.
Familiar from florists' bouquets, these cormous plants can be grown in containers for flowers in early spring. Use prepared corms of florists' freesias (some freesias can be grown in the garden and are not suitable for forcing). There are many named cultivars, bearing flowers in a range of delicate colours, but all exquisite scented. The flowers are borne on wiry, branching stems to 45cm (18in) tall from late winter to late spring. Plant the corms in late summer to early winter for spring flowers. After flowering, reduce watering gradually and store the dry corms until autumn, when they can be replanted.

### *Iris*
More often seen as early-flowering garden plants, *I. reticulata* and its cultivars can be grown in containers of well-drained compost. The typical iris flowers are fragrant and to 6cm (2½in) across. They should be planted outside after flowering.

### *Lachenalia aloides* (Cape cowslip)
Formerly known as *L. tricolor*, these bulbous perennials have sturdy stems, to 30cm (1ft) tall, hung with rows of narrow, yellow bells with green and red markings. The arching, strap-shaped leaves have contrast markings. These plants are native to South Africa and will not survive in the garden in cooler areas. Flowers appear from winter to early spring from bulbs planted in late summer.

### *Lilium*
There are many lovely lily cultivars that can be grown in containers, and they are a beautiful addition to a conservatory or cool greenhouse. Colours range from pure white to gleaming reds and yellows, and many lilies are sweetly scented. After flowering and during the dormant period, lilies can be propagated by removing scales, offset or bulblets.

### *Nerine*
The genus contains the familiar and hardy *N. bowdenii*, but *N. flexuosa*, also from South Africa, is tender. In late autumn the bulbs produce whorls of flowers with backward curving, pink petals on stems to 45cm (18in) tall; 'Alba' has white flowers. The flowers are followed by attractive grass-like leaves. Plant bulbs in late summer. *N. sarniensis* (Guernsey lily) is similar to *N. flexuosa*, but the flowers have narrower petals in white, orange or red and are borne on stems to 45cm (18in) tall.

# 8 PROPAGATION

Growing your own plants, whether from seed or by one of the vegetative methods, such as cuttings or layering, is an immensely satisfying pastime.

*Left*: Growing your own plants from seed, from bulbs or by dividing plants is not only satisfying, but is an excellent means of obtaining large displays of plants at relatively little expense.
*Right:* Although *Streptocarpus* (Cape primrose) can be grown from seed, they are unlikely to come true to type, so vegetative propagation is the best way of ensuring that new plants are like the parent plant.

Of the many plants that can be raised from seed it could be best to begin with flowering annuals. Most seeds are available only in fairly large quantities, but you cannot have too many summer-flowering *Impatiens* (busy Lizzie) and *Schizanthus* (butterfly plant), *Thunbergia* (black-eyed Susan) and *Calceolaria* (slipper flower) – and, if you find you have, there will be no problem in finding homes for the spares. Few houseplant annuals are generally available as bought plants, and it is certainly much cheaper to raise your own.

Short-lived pot plants, such as *Primula sinensis* (Chinese primrose) and *P. malacoides* (fairy primrose), give extra pleasure at reduced cost when you have raised them from seed. Move on to the rarer plants, such as some of the succulents and cacti, and once you have started to raise these you will be hooked.

Plants can be grown from cuttings, by dividing the roots or by growing on small plantlets and offsets produced by the parent plant. These are known as

vegetative means of propagation. When you grow plants from seed you cannot always be sure exactly what the results will be, because, except with F1 hybrids, nature is free to choose some of the details, such as exact flower colour or markings. Vegetative propagation methods allow you to reproduce the parent plant exactly, so that you get a miniature replica of it. Taking leaf cuttings, for example, is a form of vegetative propagation. It involves detaching leaves from a parent plant and encouraging roots to form on them. Some leaf cuttings are taken from whole leaves, while others are cut into squares, triangles or cross-sections. Early to midsummer is the best time to encourage roots to form on leaves, thereby ensuring that young plants are well established by autumn.

Succulent plants are popular and, once established, are ideal for brightening sunny windowsills throughout the year. They tolerate extremes of temperature better than any other type of plant. Many of these plants can

be raised from seeds and are sold in mixtures or individual species, but a much quicker way to produce replicas of a plant is to grow new ones from cuttings.

Division is an easy way to increase some congested houseplants, and if they are not split into exceptionally small pieces there is an opportunity to produce several attractive plants instantly. Always use young, healthy pieces from around the outside of a clump; discard old parts from its centre. Houseplants that can be increased in this way include *Saintpaulia* (African violet), *Spathiphyllum wallisii* (peace lily), *Maranta* (prayer plant), many ferns and some succulents. Cane cuttings are thick pieces of bare stem from plants with cane-like stems, such as yuccas and cordylines, cut into small lengths and either inserted vertically into or pressed on the surface of well-drained compost. They offer a good way to increase plants that are bare of leaves and so unattractive that otherwise they might have to be thrown away.

# sowing seed

To grow plants from seed you must provide somewhere where seed trays can be kept in warmth at a fairly constant temperature, in good light, undisturbed and away from draughts, and when you pot up seedlings the pots will take up quite a lot of room. Otherwise, little equipment is needed and you certainly do not need a greenhouse – a sunny spare room or even a kitchen windowsill is ideal.

Use small trays (seed pans) for small quantities of seed and standard seed trays for larger quantities. Trays should be washed and scrubbed clean. Keep each container for seeds of one species only as the plants grow at different rates, and use plastic labels and waterproof ink to label the trays.

Check the compost every day, without disturbing the tray. Water it from below when necessary to keep it constantly moist but not wet. Keep the trays in a draught-free place and at an even temperature. If there is no specific recommendation on the packet, maintain them at 16–21°C (61–70°F).

Keep seeds that germinate best in the dark in a cupboard or place a folded newspaper over the glass or propagator lid until the seedlings appear. As soon as this happens give the seedlings good light (but not strong sunlight) and remove the glass cover or polythene bag or open the ventilators of the propagator to allow fresh air in. Remove the cover altogether as seedlings grow. When the seedlings are large enough to handle, they should be pricked out.

## GROWING PLANTS FROM SEED

**1** Place a layer of peat or peat substitute in the tray. Clay trays and pans should be soaked for 24 hours and lined with small, clean crocks. Top with seed compost, which is light and sterile and contains well-balanced nutrients at the correct strength. Firm in the compost, carefully packing it into the corners and all around the edges.

**2** Add more compost to fill the tray completely. Smooth and level the surface by passing a straight piece of wood over it. Firm down the compost with the flat of your hand, a jam jar or a convenient piece of wood cut to the right size. When firmed the compost should come to about 2cm (¾in) below the edge of the tray.

**3** Fold a piece of paper in half and pour the seeds into the V. Tap the edge of the paper gently to spread the seeds finely and evenly over the compost. Avoid sprinkling the seeds too close to the edges because the compost dries out quickly there. Label the tray with the name of the plant and the date.

**5** Water the compost by standing the tray in a dish filled so that the water comes half way up the sides of the tray. Leave the tray in the container until water appears on the surface of the compost to make sure that the compost is evenly wet. Remove the tray and allow all excess water to drain away. If your seed tray is part of a propagator place the lid over the tray. Leave the cover on the tray until seedlings appear.

**7** As soon as the seedlings are big enough to be handled, transfer them to another tray. Prepare a tray of compost and firm it as before. Have ready a wad of wet newspaper on which to stand the seedlings so that the roots do not dry out. Use a plant label or a fork to 'dig' up small clumps of seedlings. Separate them, taking care not to handle the roots, which are easily damaged, but hold them gently by their leaves.

**4** Most seeds germinate better when covered with a thin layer of compost (check the seed packet for details). Sprinkle a fine layer of compost over the surface by passing it through a sieve. The layer should be three or four times the diameter of the seeds. Only the finest sprinkling is needed for small seeds.

**6** If you do not use a propagator you can slide the seed tray into a polythene bag, and tie loosely with a tag. Alternatively, cover the top with a sheet of glass, making sure that it does not actually touch the compost. Cover seeds that germinate in the dark with newspaper. Remove the glass or polythene every day and wipe off the condensation before replacing it.

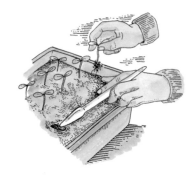

**8** Use a pencil or small dibber make holes in the new compost, spaced 4–5cm (1½–2in) apart. Drop the seedlings into the holes one by one, handling them gently, and firm them in with their seed 'leaves' just above the compost surface. Water from below and allow to drain as before. Keep the tray in bright light (but not strong sun). True leaves will develop as the seedlings grow. Pot plants into individual pots when their leaves show signs of beginning to touch.

# taking cuttings

Propagating plants from cuttings can be a good way to grow replacements for short-lived plants and much-loved plants which are outgrowing their space. It can also, of course, be an ideal way to increase the numbers of plants of which you would like more. By way of equipment you need nothing more than clean flowerpots, a sharp knife, cuttings compost, which is well aerated and well draining but also moisture retentive, a polythene bag and a few short sticks to support it.

Mists, hormone rooting powder and propagating units are optional extras, and you must provide a light place with an even temperature of 13–18°C (55–64°F), or more for tropical plants. Several cuttings can be grown in one pot.

## TIP CUTTINGS

Select a healthy specimen with plenty of well-developed stems, taken from the outside of the plant. Soft new growth does not readily root. Water the plant well the day before taking cuttings. Keep the cuttings in good light (but not direct sun) and steady warmth until new growth indicates that roots have formed. Then remove polythene and pot the plants on in potting compost. Pinch them out at the growing points as they grow to encourage bushy growth.

**1** Use a sharp knife, scalpel or craft knife to cut a 8–13cm (3–5in) length of stem, with a growing tip at the end. Make the cut just above a leaf joint (node) and cut it at an angle sloping away from the joint.

**2** Trim the stem, cutting it off just below the bottom of the leaf joint (the point from which new roots develop). Cleanly slice off the lower leaf or pairs of leaves. If preparing several cuttings keep in water until all are ready.

### *Rooting cuttings in water*

*African violet leaf petiole cuttings can be rooted in water. Cover the top of a bottle with kitchen paper, held in place with a rubber band. Pierce a hole it and insert the cutting. Keep it warm, light and draught-free, ensuring the end remains in water, until roots develop. Tear away the paper, remove the cutting and pot it up in a small pot.*

**3** Make a hole in a pot of compost. Dip the cutting in rooting powder. Insert it in the compost, making sure the leaves are not touching it.

**4** Water the compost from above. To conserve moisture make a 'tent' around the cutting with a polythene bag (with holes for air) supported on split canes.

## TAKING STEM CUTTINGS

Plants such as *Hedera* spp. (ivy), and others which have long, trailing, woody stems with leaves growing at intervals along their whole length can be propagated from stem cuttings taken from a length of stem, without the need for growing tips on the individual cuttings.

One long piece of stem is divided into several cuttings that can be planted up into pots of cuttings compost, watered in and covered in a polythene 'tent' until new growth appears, indicating that the young cuttings have taken root and can safely be potted on.

## LEAF PETIOLE CUTTINGS

A leaf petiole cutting uses a leaf and its stalk (the petiole). Soft-stemmed plants root particularly well in this way, and the method is often used for *Saintpaulia* (African violet).

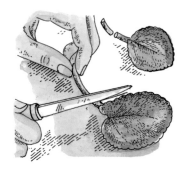

**1** Cut off a good length of young, supple stem, using a sharp knife. Cutting just above the leaf joints, divide the stems into small pieces, each with a leaf.

**3** Water the pot, then cover with a 'tent' of polythene as for tip cuttings, making sure that the leaves do not touch the polythene.

**1** Choose a plant with plenty of leaves, and make sure that the leaves you select have firm, fleshy petioles. Cut off leaf stalks at the base, using a sharp knife. Trim down the stems so that they are 3–4cm (1¼–1½in) long.

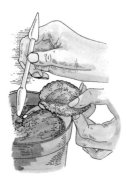

**2** Insert the cuttings into a pot of cuttings compost, several to a pot, using a pencil or dibber to make the holes. Avoid placing the cuttings too close to the edges of the pot where compost quickly becomes dry.

**4** When small new leaves appear the cuttings have rooted and should be transferred to separate small pots of potting compost.

**2** Dip the petiole tips in hormone rooting powder and insert the cuttings in a pot of cuttings compost, using a dibber or pencil to make the holes. Firm in the cuttings and stand the pot in water, to make sure the leaves do not get wet. Put the pot in a polythene 'tent' and keep it warm until new growth appears.

# leaf cuttings

Before severing a leaf, water the parent plant thoroughly several times, preferably during the previous day so that the leaf is full of water and will not deteriorate before roots have formed. Check that the leaf is healthy, pest- and disease-free and a good copy of the parent plant. Each leaf used as a cutting should be relatively young and without surfaces that have become hard and old. These do not root rapidly.

After the cuttings have been inserted in compost, position them out of strong and direct sunlight; small leaf-squares and triangles soon shrivel when in strong sunlight. It is better to place them on a cool, well-shaded windowsill than on a sunny one. Keep the compost moist during rooting. As soon as roots and shoots develop, remove the plastic covering and lower the temperature.

## WHOLE-LEAF CUTTINGS

Plants such as the *Begonia rex, B. masoniana* (iron-cross begonia) and cultivars of *Streptocarpus* (Cape primrose) can be increased from whole-leaf cuttings, a means of propagating a number of plantlets from one leaf.

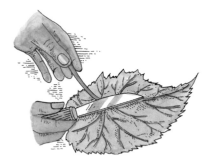

**1** Sever the stalk of a healthy leaf close to its base, taking care not to leave a short snag on the plant that later would die back. Place the severed leaf upside down on a wooden board and cut off the stalk, close to the leaf.

**2** Use a sharp knife to make cuts, 20–25mm (¾–1in) apart, across the main and secondary veins, taking care not to cut completely through the leaf.

**3** Place the leaf vein-side down on equal parts moist peat and sharp sand. Use small stones or pieces of U-shaped wire, inserted astride the veins, to hold the leaf in contact with the compost.

**4** Lightly water the compost, allow excess moisture to evaporate, then cover with a transparent lid. Put in gentle warmth and light shade. When the young plants are large enough, transfer them to pots.

## LEAF SECTIONS

In addition to positioning whole leaf cuttings on the surface of compost, cultivars of *Streptocarpus* (Cape primrose) can be increased by severing leaves into sections. Sever a healthy leaf and place it on a flat board. Use a sharp knife to cut it laterally into pieces about 5cm (2in) wide. Use the blade of a knife to make 2cm (¾in) deep slits in the compost, into which cuttings can be inserted and firmed.

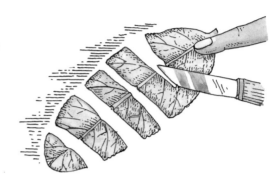

## LEAF TRIANGLES

These are easier to insert in compost than leaf squares, and they tend to be slightly larger, which gives them a greater reserve of food while they are developing their roots. Water a mother plant and the following day remove a healthy leaf. Sever it close to the plant's base and then again next to the leaf. Place the leaf on a flat board and use a sharp knife to cut triangles, each with its point towards the position where the stalk joined it. Fill and firm a seed tray with equal parts moist peat and sharp sand. Use a knife to make slits into which cuttings can be inserted to half their depth with the point facing down. Firm the compost around them and place in light shade and gentle warmth.

## LEAF SQUARES

Many more cuttings of this type can be taken from an individual leaf than the triangular type (see below). After severing a leaf from a healthy plant, cut off the stalk and place the leaf on a board. Cut it into strips about 3cm (1¼in) wide, each with a main or secondary vein running down the middle. Then cut each of the strips into squares. Each square is inserted separately and by about one-third of its depth into equal parts of moist peat and sharp sand. It is vital that cuttings are inserted with the side that was nearest to the leafstalk facing downwards or they will not root.

Make a slit in the compost with a knife and insert a cutting. Firm the compost around it, lightly water the surface and place it in gentle warmth and light shade. Cover with a plastic, translucent lid. When the cuttings have developed plantlets, transfer them into small, individual pots. Water the compost gently and place the plantlets in light shade until they are properly established.

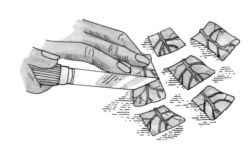

### Horizontal leaf squares

Small leaf squares can be pressed flat on the surface of compost formed of equal parts moist peat and sharp sand. These leaf cuttings are about 3cm (1¼in) square and they need to be carefully secured horizontally on the compost's surface. Because they are small, hooked pieces of wire are easier to use than pebbles.

# cane cuttings

This type of cutting involves cutting bare stems into pieces 8–13cm (3–5in) long and either inserting them vertically into pots of sandy compost or pressing them horizontally on the surface. Plants like yucca and dieffenbachia can be are increased in this way. Specially prepared cuttings of yucca are sometimes available; these can be inserted vertically into cuttings compost and kept at a gentle, even temperature until roots form and shoots appear.

Old plants of dieffenbachia often have several long, bare stems that have small tufts of leaves at their top. Instead of discarding these plants, cut their stems into pieces about 8cm (3in) long. When you handle dieffenbachia either wear gloves or make sure that you do not touch your mouth and eyes if your hands have come into contact with the sap.

## TAKING CANE CUTTINGS

**1** Use a sharp knife to cut a thick, healthy stem from the congested base of a dieffenbachia. Cut low down to ensure that an unsightly stub does not remain, and take care not to damage the plant.

**2** Cut the stem into several pieces, each about 8cm (3in) long. Make sure that each length has at least one strong, healthy bud to create good upward growth and develop into healthy new shoots.

**3** Fill a wide pot with equal parts moist peat and sharp sand and firm it to 1cm (½in) below the rim. Press each cutting to half its thickness into the compost and secure with pieces of bent wire.

**4** Water the compost, allow to drain and place a plastic dome over the pot. Alternatively, insert small pieces of split cane around the pot's edge and draw a plastic bag over. Secure it with an elastic band.

# division

One of the easiest ways of increasing some overcrowded houseplants is by division.

*Saintpaulia* (African violet), for example, are easily increased by removing congested plants from their pots and teasing them apart. Tap the edge of a congested pot on a hard corner to remove the rootball. Gently pull the plants apart and repot the young pieces into small, individual pots. Water the compost gently from below.

Plants that have variegated leaves, such as *Sansevieria trifasciata* 'Laurentii', have to be propagated by division if the variegation is to be maintained as they will not breed true.

## DIVIDING SANSEVIERIAS

**1** A plant such as sansevieria will eventually fills its pot with fibrous roots, with many stems and leaves arising directly from the roots. When the rootball completely fills the pot, the quality of the plant's leaves deteriorates. At this point, it becomes necessary to divide the plant. Water the compost the day before dividing it to make sure that the roots, stems and leaves are full of moisture. Dehydrated plants are less likely to survive division than those that have been well watered.

**2** Invert the plant and knock the pot's rim on a corner of a hard surface. As you ease out the plant, support the rootball, so that it gently slides from the pot but does not break up or fall on the floor. Using your fingers, gently tease and pull apart the rootball, dividing it into several substantially sized pieces. It may be necessary to cut through some roots, but you should never just slice through the rootball. Discard old pieces from the plant's centre and use only young, outer parts.

**3** Select a clean pot, slightly smaller than before but large enough to accommodate the roots. Place compost in its base and position a divided piece in the centre. Hold the plant so that the soil-mark which indicates its earlier depth in a pot is about 1cm (½in) below the pot's rim. Then, gently trickle compost around the roots, spreading it evenly and in layers. Fill and firm compost to within 1cm (½in) of the rim, then lightly but thoroughly water it. Allow excess moisture to drain.

# runners & plantlets

Many houseplants produce plantlets or offsets from which new plants can be grown. Some send out runners or stolons (creeping stems), which travel along the ground, developing tiny new plants that root in the soil. Others develop roots along their arching stems, wherever these touch the ground. These can be pegged down into the ground along their length to encourage rooting. In houseplants stolons and their little plantlets can be an attractive feature of the plant and are usually left to hang. Other plants produce their plantlets around, and attached to, the parent, and these miniature plants, usually known as offsets,
can be detached and grown on. Some plantlets begin to produce their own roots while hanging on the plant, while others develop them when they come in contact with a suitable growing medium.

## TRAILING OFFSETS

*Chlorophytum comosum* (spider plant) and *Saxifraga stolonifera* (mother of thousands) are among the easiest plants to grow from offsets. Both produce small versions of themselves at the end of long, arching stems. Stand the plant on a tray and surround it with small pots of cutting or potting compost. Water them all. Arch the stolons over so that the plantlets are resting on the
surface of the compost, one per pot. Use a hairpin or a piece of bent wire to anchor each stolon in place. Keep the compost moist, and sever the stolons when new growth appears.

## DETACHABLE OFFSETS

Some plants have offsets that grow on the plant itself, either on the leaf surface or (more usually) around the rosettes of leaves that form the plant. These offsets can be severed from the parent plant and grown on. Typical are *Kalanchoe delagoensis* (syn. *K. tubiflora*; chandelier plant), with offsets that grow at the leaf tips, and *K. daigremontiana* (syn. *Bryophyllum daigremontianum*; Mexican hat plant, devil's backbone), in which they grow around the leaf edges.

## OTHER OFFSETS

Many succulents and bromeliads have offsets that grow on, or around the base of, the plant. Sometimes these are easily identifiable as new plants, as in many of the cacti, while in other cases they are attached to the parent, as in many bromeliads. The best time to remove the offsets is during repotting. Cut them off with a sharp clean knife; for those growing up around the base, try to make sure that you get a bit of root. Allow cactus offsets to dry for a few days before planting them in cactus compost, but pot up other plants in potting compost straight away. Half-fill the pot first and hold the plant with the roots in the pot as you trickle in more compost. Firm in and water from below.

## ROOTING DETACHABLE OFFSETS

**1** Water the parent plant the day before taking offsets. Fill an 8cm (3in) pot with potting compost and water it. Remove only a few plantlets from each leaf with your fingers or tweezers (to avoid altering the appearance of the plant), handling them carefully.

**2** Arrange the plantlets on the surface of the compost, so that each has its own growing space. Keep the compost moist by watering from below. When the plants grow, roots will have formed and they should be potted in individual pots.

# layering

Propagating from runners and arching stems is called layering, and *Hedera* spp. (ivy) and other climbers can be reproduced in this way. The method produces a replica of the parent plant, so a healthy parent is essential. Water the plant well the day before.

Place a pot filled with cuttings compost next to the parent plant. Fold over a stem (without cutting it off) near a node, about 15cm (6in) from the tip, to form a V in the stem and anchor the V of the stem into the compost with bent wire. Firm compost over the V and water the compost from above. Keep the compost moist as new roots develop. When fresh growth appears at the tip of the stem, this indicates that roots have formed; sever the new plant from its parent with a sharp knife or scissors.

## AIR LAYERING

This is an ideal way to give a tall, leggy plant that has lost its lower leaves a new lease of life, and it is often used on *Ficus elastica* (rubber plant), and sometimes on dieffenbachias, dracaenas and monsteras. Air layering involves encouraging roots to develop just below the lowest leaf; when these are established the stem is severed and the plant is re-potted. This is not a rapid method of propagation.

**1** Water the plant the day before. Use a sharp knife to make an upward-slanting cut, two-thirds through the stem and 8–10cm (3–4in) below the lowest leaf. Take care that the top of the plant does not bend and snap. Use a matchstick to keep the surfaces of the cut apart. If they are allowed to close, the wound heals and does not readily develop roots. Trim off the ends of the matchstick and use a small brush to coat the plant's cut surfaces with hormone rooting powder and push powder into the cut.

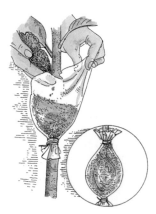

**2** Wind a piece of polythene around the stem with the cut area in the centre. Use strong string to tie it about 5cm (2in) below the cut, winding the string around several times to hold it.

**3** Carefully fill the polythene with moist peat. Fill the tube to within 8cm (3in) of the top, then tie it off. Place the plant in gentle warmth and light shade. Check that the peat is moist fortnightly.

**4** Within two months roots show through the polythene. While they are still white, cut the stem below the the tube. Remove the polythene and string and retain as much peat as possible. Pot up.

*Left*: Place cactus cuttings in gentle warmth and light shade. Rooting should occur in a few weeks in spring and early summer.

# propagating cacti & other succulents

There are various ways of taking cuttings of succulent plants. One method is to cut a leaf into sections; sometimes whole leaves are rooted; and cacti are grown from short stubs. Take care when detaching leaves that the mother plant's shape is not ruined; a few leaves removed from the back of a plant usually does no harm and passes unnoticed.

**LEAF DIVISION**

Some large plants, such as *Sansevieria trifasciata*, can be increased by cutting stems or leaves into pieces.

**1** Water the plant well a few days before severing the leaves because flaccid leaves do not readily root. Use a sharp knife to sever one or two leaves at their base. Do not take all of them from one side, as this will mar the plant's shape.

**2** Place the leaf on a flat surface and use a sharp knife to cut it into pieces about 5cm (2in) deep. Cut cleanly because torn surfaces do not root readily.

**3** Fill and firm a shallow but wide pot with equal parts moist peat and sharp sand. Form a slit with a knife, then push a cutting about 2cm (¾in) into it. Make sure that the cutting is the right way up. Lightly water the compost and place in gentle warmth.

## SMALL AND CIRCULAR LEAVES

Several succulents have small, circular and flat leaves. These include *Sedum sieboldii* and *S. s.* 'Mediovariegatum'. These are easily increased in spring and early summer by pressing leaves into the surface of well-drained compost formed of equal parts moist peat and sharp sand. Cut off entire stems, rather than removing a few leaves from several shoots.

Snap off the leaves, taking care not to squash them. Leave them to dry for a couple of days. Press individual leaves on the compost's surface, then lightly water them. Place the pot in gentle warmth and light shade.

## WHOLE-LEAF CUTTINGS

The leaves of some succulents, such as *Crassula ovata* (jade plant), can be removed and inserted vertically into well-drained compost in spring and early summer. High temperatures are not necessary. Select a healthy, well-watered plant and gently bend the leaves down so they snap off close to the main stem. Leave them to dry for a couple of days. Fill a clean pot with equal parts moist peat and sharp sand and firm it to about 1cm (½in) below the rim. Form a hole 20mm (¾in) deep and insert a cutting in it. Firm compost around it. Water and put the pot in light shade and gentle warmth.

## CACTUS CUTTINGS

Most cacti are known for their spines, but this should not stop cuttings being taken. If necessary, wear a pair of thin rubber kitchen gloves. Cacti that create a mass of small stems from around their base are easily increased from cuttings. Mammillarias and *Echinopsis* spp. can be increased in this way.

**1** Use a sharp knife to remove well-formed young stems from around the outside of the clump. Sever the stems directly at their base so that unsightly short stubs of growth are not left on the mother plant. Do not take them all from the same position to avoid spoiling the plant's appearance.

**2** Leave the cuttings for a couple of days so that their ends can dry before inserting in cactus compost. This allows them to root much more quickly than if inserted immediately after being severed.

**3** Fill a small pot with equal parts moist peat and sharp sand and firm it to 1cm (½in) below the rim. Sprinkle a thin layer of sharp sand on the surface and use a small dibber to make a hole about 2.5cm (1in) deep, into which a cutting can be inserted. Firm compost around its base. Lightly water the compost. Place cuttings in gentle warmth and light shade. Rooting takes a few weeks in spring and early summer.

# 9 TROUBLESHOOTING

Unlike plants grown outdoors, houseplants are in artificial surroundings: their roots are confined in a small amount of compost that can be easily excessively watered or underwatered; they are frequently exposed to high temperatures even though the intensity of light is poor; and the temperature may fluctuate rapidly throughout the day and, in winter, be cold at night when heating systems are turned down or off. It is remarkable, therefore, that so many houseplants succeed and this is invariably due to the enthusiasm and vigilance of houseplant growers.

*Opposite:* Many problems with plants can be avoided by putting them in the right situation. For example, *Cissus rhombifolia* (grape ivy) will tolerate light shade that would be too dark for *Philodendron scandens* (sweetheart plant).
*Left:* Hoyas, such as *H. carnosa* 'Tricolor' might be suitable for a bathroom in summer as they like humidity during the growing season. In the winter, however, they may need a drier atmosphere with a more even temperature.

Pests and diseases soon devastate houseplants if they remain undetected or neglected. Leaves, stems, shoots and flowers can all be affected, as well as roots. Prevention is easier than trying to eliminate an established colony of pests or a severe infection of a disease. Buying only clean and healthy plants reduces the risk of most pests or diseases infecting your plants. If you are doubtful about the health of a plant, isolate it for a couple of weeks before introducing it into a room where there are other plants. When watering plants, cleaning leaves or removing dead flowers, thoroughly inspect the plants to ensure they are clean and healthy. If a problem is noticed, treat it immediately, before other plants become affected. Use only clean potting composts and never take cuttings from infected plants.

Some of the cultural problems affecting houseplants are outlined below, and the pests and diseases most often seen are described on pages 122–3. Most houseplants underachieve and this is because they are not regularly fed. Those that are given a balanced diet have a better chance of surviving an infestation of pests or diseases than if undernourished and struggling for life. On the other hand, do not feed plants excessively, because this may make the compost toxic, which will retard growth or even kill them. Nor should you feed summer-flowering or foliage plants after late summer, because this will encourage the lush growth that is susceptible to pests and diseases, just when the plants are preparing to take a winter rest.

*Left:* Plants that might be more suited to a conservatory or cool greenhouse are best kept near a window in the home, where they can be used to provide welcome shade.

### APPLYING CHEMICALS

There are several ways in which to apply chemicals to plants: spraying with a concentrated insecticide diluted in clean water is the most popular method. Some liquid sprays are ready to use. Dusting plants is also effective, but may leave an unattractive residue. Watering compost with a systemic insecticide and using insecticidal sticks are other methods.

Inserting an insecticidal stick into compost is a quick, clean and effective way to control pests. Each stick contains a systemic insecticide that makes a plant toxic to insects.

Dusting plants with a powder is not a popular way to apply insecticides to houseplants, but it is quick and effective. When you use powder distribute it evenly and take the plant outdoors to avoid inhaling it and to protect furniture and soft furnishings.

When you apply a liquid spray put the plant inside a clean dustbin or large plastic bag. Then, apply the spray and leave the container closed for an hour.

Remove the plant and allow the fumes to disperse before replacing it indoors.

### CULTURAL PROBLEMS

In addition to being damaged by pests and diseases, plants can become unhealthy through incorrect conditions, such as too little or too much water, excessive shade or strong sunlight, inappropriate temperatures, excessive humidity or insufficient food. Some common cultural problems are detailed opposite.

## CULTURAL PROBLEMS

Variegated leaves become green if the plant is not in good light; reposition the plant near a window.

Leaves sometimes develop holes in their centre or along the outer edge. This is because they either have been knocked by people or pets, or are infested with pests such as caterpillars.

Flowers become dry and rapidly fade if compost becomes dry, the temperature is too high, the air too dry or if the plant is in dense shade.

Flower buds fall off if the compost or air is dry, the plant is in poor light or, in the case of some cacti, if the plant is moved and knocked.

Leaves curl at their edges, then fall off, if the plant is in a cold draught, the temperature is low or the compost has been excessively watered.

Leaves wilt if compost is either very wet or dry. Excessively dry air and too much heat also causes wilting. On hot days plants may temporarily wilt in the early afternoon but recover by evening.

Leaves wilt and decay if the compost is too wet. This especially applies to foliage plants in winter.

Lower leaves become dry and crisp and eventually fall off if the compost is too dry, temperatures are too high or there is too little light.

Blemishes occur on leaves for a number of reasons: burned areas appear after leaves with water droplets on their surfaces are left in strong sunlight; diseases such as leaf spot also produce holes.

A white, powdery coating on a clay pot usually indicates that the plant has been excessively fed. It also means that the water may contain a great deal of chalk.

Green slime appears on clay pots if the compost has been excessively watered. The slime may also appear on the surface of compost.

# pests & diseases

### Aphids
These soft-bodied insects, usually green, suck sap from leaves and petals, causing mottling and distortion. They excrete honeydew, which attracts sooty mould. Spray plants regularly, especially in summer.

### Caterpillars
Although they are seldom seen indoors, caterpillars do occasionally crop up in sun rooms and conservatories. They chew holes in leaves. Pick off and destroy them and spray with an insecticide. Repeat the spray as necessary.

### Cyclamen mites
These minute, spider-like pests infest plants such as cyclamen, saintpaulias and pelargoniums. They cause stunting; leaves curl and become wrinkled, and flowers become distorted and fall off. Burn infested plants.

### Earwigs
Outdoor as well as indoor plants can be affected. They are rarely seen in daytime but at night they chew leaves and flowers, causing ragged holes and edges. Check for them at night – they hide under leaves and flowers – pick off and destroy them.

### Eelworms
There are several different types of these microscopic worms, including some that infest chrysanthemums or bulbs and some that cause irregular, corky swellings on roots (root-knot eelworm). If these worms are seen on the plant, it must be burned.

### Mealy bugs
These insects resemble small woodlice but are covered in white, woolly wax. They cluster on the stems and under leaves of subtropical and tropical plants, sucking sap and causing leaves to yellow. Wipe off with cotton buds dipped in methylated spirits or alcohol.

### Red spider mites
The minute, spider-like pests that infest the undersides of leaves and suck sap, causing speckling and yellow blotches. Daily misting of leaves helps to prevent an attack. Use a systemic insecticide. Burn seriously infected plants.

### Root mealy bugs
Like mealy bugs, these resemble small woodlice, but live on the outer roots of plants in pots. They eat roots, especially of cacti and other succulents. Inspect roots, especially when plants are repotted. Drench the compost in an insecticide.

### Scale insects
The first sign of an infestation is usually when plants become sticky. Swollen, protective, waxy-brown discs appear and female scale insects produce their young under them. Wipe off with cotton buds dipped in methylated spirits or alcohol. Burn seriously infected plants.

### Thrips
These tiny, dark brown, fly-like pests have light coloured legs and wings. They jump from plant to plant, sucking leaves and flowers, causing silvery streaks and mottling. Flowers become distorted. Plants with dry compost suffer most. Spray several times with insecticide.

### Whitefly
These are small, white and moth-like and when disturbed flutter around their host plant. Their young are green, suck sap and excrete honeydew, encouraging the presence of sooty mould. Eradication is not easy; spray repeatedly with insecticide.

### Black leg

This is a disease mainly of cuttings and especially pelargoniums. The bases of stems become soft and turn black. Wet, cold, compacted and airless compost encourages it. Destroy seriously infected cuttings.

### Botrytis

Also known as grey mould, this forms a grey, furry mould on soft parts of plants, especially flowers, young leaves and shoots. It is encouraged by still, damp air. Cut off infected parts, remove dead flowers and spray with a fungicide. Create better air circulation around plants.

### Leaf spot

Especially prone to this disease are dieffenbachias, dracaenas and citrus plants. It causes black spots that enlarge and merge. Remove and burn infected leaves and spray infected plants with a fungicide.

### Powdery mildew

This produces a white, powdery coating over leaves – often on both sides. It also infects flowers and stems. Remove badly infected parts, increase ventilation and keep the surrounding air drier.

### Root rot

Sometimes known as tuber rot, this occurs on palms, cacti and other succulents, begonias and African violets. Plants wilt and leaves become yellow. It is caused by continuously waterlogged compost.

### Rust

This is uncommon on indoor plants, except for pelargoniums. Carnations and chrysanthemums in sun rooms and conservatories are sometimes infected. Raised rings of black or brown spores appear on leaves. Remove and burn infected leaves, increase ventilation and spray with a fungicide.

### Sooty mould

The black, powdery, soot-like mould lives on honeydew excreted by aphids and other sap-sucking pests. It coats leaves, stems and flowers. Spray against aphids and use a damp cloth to wipe away light infestations.

### Viruses

Microscopic particles invade plants, causing disorder but seldom killing their host. Deformed growth, mottling and streaking in leaves and colour changes in flowers are the most usual results. No treatment is possible, except to control sap-sucking insects that spread viruses.

## Safety First with Chemicals

*All chemicals used to control pests and diseases must be handled with care.*

- *Keep all chemicals out of the reach of children, and never transfer them to bottles that youngsters might believe to hold a refreshing drink.*
- *Always follow the manufacturer's instructions. Using a chemical at a higher concentration does not improve its effectiveness and may even damage plants.*
- *Some plants are allergic to certain chemicals, so check with the label, especially when spraying palms, ferns, cacti and other succulents.*
- *Never mix chemicals, unless recommended.*
- *Whenever possible, take houseplants outdoors to spray them and never use sprays in rooms where birds, fish and other pets are present.*
- *Never use chemical sprays near to food and fruit, and avoid spraying wallpaper and fabrics.*
- *Do not assume that insecticides derived from natural plant extracts are not dangerous.*

# GLOSSARY

**Acaricide** A chemical used to kill parasitic spider mites, such as red spider mites.

**Acid** Compost or soil with a pH below 7.0. Most plants grow best in slightly acid conditions, about pH 6.5.

**Adventitious roots** Roots that develop from unusual positions, such as on leaves and stems.

**Aerial roots** These are roots that appear from a stem and above soil level, as with the Swiss cheese plants (*Monstera deliciosa*), some ivies and orchids. Their prime task is to gain support for stems.

**Air layering** A method of propagating plants by encouraging roots to form on stems. The rubber plant (*Ficus elastica*) is often increased in this way.

**Alkaline** Compost or soil with a pH above 7.0.

**Alternate** Buds or leaves that grow on opposite sides of a stem or shoot.

**Annual** A plant that completes its life-cycle within a year; seeds germinate, the plant grows, and flowers and seeds are produced within one growing season.

**Anther** Part of a stamen, the male reproductive part of a flower. A stamen is formed of a stalk (filament), with an anther at its top. Pollen grains form within anthers.

**Aphids** Perhaps the main pest of house and garden plants and also known as greenfly. They breed rapidly in spring and summer, clustering around the soft parts of the flowers, shoots, stems and leaves. They suck sap, causing debilitation as well as spreading viruses.

**Apical** The tip of a shoot or branch.

**Areole** A modified sideshoot, resembling a tiny hump, unique to cacti. It bears spines, hairs, bristles or wool.

**Asexual** A non-sexual way to increase plants, such as by cuttings, layering and division rather than seed.

**Axil** The junction between a leaf and stem, from where sideshoots or flowers may develop.

**Bigeneric hybrid** A plant produced by crossing two plants from different genera. This is indicated by a cross positioned in front of the plant's name. For instance, the ivy tree (x *Fatshedera lizei*) is a cross between a form of the false castor oil plant (*Fatsia japonica* 'Moderi' – also known as the Japanese fatsia), and the Irish ivy (*Hedera helix* 'Hibernica').

**Bloom** This has two meanings, either flowers or a powdery coating on flowers, stems or leaves.

**Bottle gardening** Growing plants in environments created by carboys and other large glass jars. Sometimes the container is stoppered and the air inside recycled by plants, while in other cases, the container is left open.

**Bract** A modified leaf; some provide protection for a flower while others assume the role of petals and are the main attraction. Poinsettia (*Euphorbia pulcherrima*) has brightly coloured bracts.

**Bromeliad** A member of the Bromeliaceae family. Many have rosettes of leaves that form urns. A few of them are epiphytes.

**Bulb** A storage organ with a bud-like structure. It is formed of fleshy scales attached at their base to a flattened stem called the basal plate.

**Bulbil** An immature and miniature bulb that usually grows at the base of another bulb. However, some plants, such as the mother fern (*Asplenium bulbiferum*), develop plantlets on their leaves which are also known as bulbils. These can be detached carefully using tweezers and encouraged to form roots.

**Cactus** A succulent plant belonging to the Cactaceae family. All cacti are characterized by having areoles.

**Capillary action** The passage of water upwards through potting compost ro soil. The finer the soil particles, the higher the rise of moisture. The same principle is used in self-watering systems for plants in pots in sun rooms, conservatories and greenhouses.

**Chlorophyll** Green pigment in plants that captures the energy in sunlight and allow the process of photosynthesis.

**Clone** A plant raised vegetatively from another plant, so ensuring that it is identical in every particular to the parent.

**Columnar** Describes a plant that rises vertically; usually used to refer to trees and conifers but also to describe some cacti.

**Compost** In the context of houseplants refers to the medium in which plants grow when in pots or other containers, and in North America is known as potting compost. It is formed of a mixture of loam, sharp sand and peat, plus fertilizers, or peat and fertilizers.

**Corolla** The ring of petals in a flower that create the main display.

**Corona** Petals in certain plants that form a cup or trumpet, as in daffodils.

**Cristate** Crested, used to describe some ferns and cacti, as well as a few forms of houseplants.

**Crock** A piece of broken clay pot put in the base of a clay pot to prevent compost blocking the drainage hole.

**Cultivar** A variety raised in cultivation by selective breeding.

**Cutting** A vegetative method of propagating plants by which a severed piece of a plant is encouraged to develop roots.

**Damping down** Increasing the humidity in a sun room, conservatory or greenhouse by using a fine-rosed watering-can to spray water on the floor and around plants. It is best carried out early in the day so that excess moisture dries by nightfall.

**Dead-heading** The removal of faded and dead flowers to encourage the development of further flowers. It also helps to prevent deseases infecting decaying flowers.

**Dibber** A rounded, blunt-pointed tool for making planting holes in compost.

**Division** A vegetative method of propagation, involving dividing the stems and roots of plants.

**Dormancy** The resting period of a plant or seed.

**Double flowers** Flowers with more than the normal number of petals.

**Drawn** Describes thin and spindly shoots or plants, after having been grown in crowded or dark conditions.

**Epiphyte** A plant that grows above ground level, attached to trees, rocks and, sometimes, other plants. Epiphytes do not take nourishment from their hosts, but just use them for support. Many orchids and bromeliads are epiphytes.

**Ericaceous compost** Acidic potting medium, suitable for such plants as azaleas.

**Etiolated** Blanched and spindly, the result of being grown in poor light.

**F1** The first filial generation and the result of a cross between two pure-bred and unrelated parents. F1 hybrids are large, strong and uniform, but their seeds will not produce replicas of the parents.

**Fern** A perennial, flowerless plant that produces spores.

**Fertilization** The sexual union of male (pollen) and female (ovule) parts.

**Filament** the slender stalk that supports the anthers of a flower.

Collectively, the anthers and filaments form the stamen.

**Fimbriate** Fringed and usually referring to a flower or petal.

**Flore-pleno** Refers to flowers with a larger than normal number of petals.

**Floret** A small flower that, with others, forms a flower head, such as in chrysanthemums and other members of the Compositae family.

**Frond** Leaf of a palm or fern.

**Fungicide** A chemical used to eradicate or deter fungal diseases.

**Germination** The process that occurs within a seed when given moisture, air and warmth. The seed's coat ruptures and a seed leaf (or seed leaves) grows towards the light, while a root grows downwards.

**Glaucous** Greyish-green or bluish-green and usually applied to describe stems, leaves or fruits.

**Glochid** Describes a small, hooked hair growing on some cacti.

**Inflorescence** Part of a plant that bears flowers.

**Insectivorous** Describes plants that are adapted to trap, kill and digest insects such as small flies. In this way they are able to supplement food that their environment is not able to provide.

**Joint** The junction of a shoot and stem, or a leaf and a leaf-stalk. These are also known as nodes.

**Juvenile leaf** Several houseplants have, when young, differently shaped leaves from those on mature plants.

**Layering** A vegetative way to increase plants, involving lowering stems and slightly burying them in soil or compost. By creating a kind, twist, bend or slit in the part of the stem that is buried, the flow of sap is restricted and roots are encouraged to develop.

**Leaflet** Some leaves are formed of several small leaves, each known as a leaflet. A leaflet is characterized by not having a bud in its axil.

**Leggy** Describes plants that have become tall and spindly, often through being kept in dark places.

**Neutral** Compost that is neither acid nor alkaline and with a pH of 7.0. Horticultural neutral is considered to be between 6.5 and 7.0.

**Node** A leaf-joint or position where a shoot grows from a stem or branch.

**Ovary** The female part of a flower where fertilization takes place and seeds grow.

**Peat** Partly decomposed vegetable material, usually with an acid nature.

Because of its capacity to retain water it is used in seed and potting composts. Substitutes are now preferred because of the rapid destruction of peat bogs.

**Perennial** Usually used when referring to herbaceous perennials, but also applied to plants that live for several years, such as trees and shrubs.

**Petiole** A leaf-stalk.

**Photosynthesis** The food-building process when chlorophyll in leaves is activated by sunlight and, together with moisture absorbed by roots and carbon dioxide absorbed through stomata from the atmosphere, creates growth.

**pH** A logarithmic scale used to define the acidity or alkalinity of a soil/water solution. The scale ranges from 0 to 14: neutral is 7.0, with figures above indicating increasing alkalinity and, below, increasing acidity.

**Pinching out** Removing the tip of a shoot to encourage the development of sideshoots.

**Plantlet** An offset produced on a plant's leaves or stem.

**Pot-bound** Describes a plant that completely fills its pot with roots and needs repotting.

**Potting on** Transferring an established plant from one pot to another.

**Potting up** Transferring a young plant from a seed tray into a pot.

**Pricking oou** Transferring seedlings from the seed tray in which they were sown into other seed trays and giving them wider spacing.

**Propagation** The raising of new plants.

**Pseudobulb** The thickened stem of some orchids.

**Rhizome** A thick underground stem that enables a plant to spread through the soil. It may also be used for food storage.

**Root-ball** The packed ball of roots and compost in which a houseplant grows.

**Root hair** The fine, feeding roots that develop on roots to absorb nutrients.

**Seed leaf** The first leaf (sometimes two) that appears after germination.

**Seedling** A young plant produced after a seed germinates.

**Self-coloured** Flowers with just one colour, in contrast to bicoloured (two colours) and multicoloured (several shades).

**Sessile** Leaves and flowers that do not have a stalk or stem attaching them to the plant.

**Softwood cutting** A cutting formed of a non-woody shoot.

**Spadix** A dense spike of tiny flowers, usually enclosed in a spathe.

**Spathe** A large bract or pair of bracts, often brightly coloured, surrounding a spadix.

**Spores** The reproductive cells of non-flowering plants.

**Stamen** The male part of a flower.

**Stigma** The female part of a flower.

**Stipule** Leaf-like sheaths at the base of some flower stalks.

**Stolon** Horizontally growing stem that roots at the nodes, as in *Saxifraga stolonifera*.

**Stomata** Minute holes – usually in the underside of a leaf – that enable an exchange of gases between the plant and the surrounding air.

**Stop** The removal of a growing tip to encourage the development of sideshoots.

**Style** Part of the female reproductive element of a flower, linking the stigma to the ovary.

**Succulent** Any plant with thick and fleshy leaves. Cacti are succulent plants, but not all succulents are cacti.

**Systemic pesticide** Describes chemicals that enter a plant's tissue, killing sucking and biting insects.

**Tendril** A thread-like growth that enables some climbers to cling to their supports.

**Terrarium** A glass container, partly or wholly enclosed, used to house plants.

**Terrestrial** Describes plants that grow in soil at ground level.

**Top dressing** Replacing the surface soil of plants in large containers with fresh potting compost, rather than transferring them into an even larger container.

**Turgid** Describes a leaf or plant that is firm and full of moisture.

**Variegated** Describes leaves of more than one colour.

**Variety** A natural occurring variation within a species. The term is also commonly used to include both true varieties and variations created by people, which are correctly termed cultivars.

**Vegetative propagation** Methods of increasing plants, including the division of roots, layering, air-layering and taking cuttings.

**Xerophytic** Describes plants adapted for living in dry climates, such as desert cacti; they are commonly characterized by slow growth, swollen storage tissues and spines.

# INDEX

# ACKNOWLEDGEMENTS

**Garden Picture Library**/A.I. Lord 90 left, /Linda Burgess 79, /Friedrich Strauss 5 detail 3, 5 detail 4, 28, 38, 41, 86 left, 87, /Steve Wooster 42

**Octopus Publishing Group Limited**/Guy Ryecart 9, 10, 14, 21, 24 top right, 24 bottom right, 26 bottom, 27 top left, 29 top, 30 left, 30 right, 34 left, 39, 43 left, 43 right, 45 right, 46, 48, 49 top, 50 left, 51 right, 53 left, 55, 56, 57, 58, 60 right, 62 right, 63, 67 top left, 67 bottom, 69 top left, 73, 74, 75 top, 75 bottom, 77 top, 77 bottom, 81 bottom, 82 bottom, 83, 85 right, 89, 90 top right, 91, 94, 95, 96 left, 96 right, 97 left, 98, 99 left, 99 right, 100, 102, 103 left, 103 right, 116, /Marianne Majerus 5 detail 2, 5 detail 7, 22, 47, 92, /Ian Wallace 97 right, /Steve Wooster 2–3, 4–5, 5 detail 1, 5 detail 6, 7, 8, 11, 12, 13, 15, 16, 18, 20, 23, 24 left, 25, 26 top, 27 right, 31, 32, 33 top, 33 bottom, 34 right, 35, 36, 37, 40, 44, 45 left, 49 bottom, 50 right, 51 left, 52, 53 right, 59, 61, 62 left, 64, 66, 67 top right, 68, 69 top right, 70, 71, 72, 76, 78, 80, 81 top, 82 top, 84, 85 left, 86 right, 88, 101, 105, 119

**Harpur Garden Library** 90 bottom right

**The Interior Archive**/Fritz von der Schulenburg 5 detail 8, 104

**Andrew Lawson** 29 bottom, 60 left

**Elizabeth Whiting & Associates** 5 detail 5, 5 detail 9, 54, 118, 120

*Cover Photography:*
**Garden Picture Library**/Steve Wooster  front cover top left
**Octopus Publishing Group Limited**/Steve Wooster front cover top right, front cover bottom

Executive Editor: Julian Brown
Editorial Manager: Jane Birch
Senior Designer: Peter Burt
Designer: Anthony Cohen
Picture Research: Christine Junemann
Production Controller: Ian Paton